Old Times, Evil Times

Memoirs

About Life Under Two Autocratic
Regimes

Second Edition

J. Endrényi

Old Times, Evil Times
Memoirs

iUniverse books may be ordered through booksellers or by contacting:

iUniverse
1663 Liberty Drive
Bloomington, IN 47403
www.iuniverse.com
1-800-Authors (1-800-288-4677)

Because of the dynamic nature of the Internet, any Web addresses or links contained in this book may have changed since publication and may no longer be valid.

ISBN: 978-1-4502-0159-9 (sc)
ISBN: 978-1-4502-0161-2 (hc)
ISBN: 978-1-4502-0160-5 (e)

Print information available on the last page.

iUniverse rev. date: 10/31/2016

Contents

Preface

This is not an autobiography. Neither is it a study of a period in history. It is a description of how the fate of a group of common people, including me and my family, was affected by events before, during, and after that horrible cataclysm, the Second World War. Anything that is normally the material of biographies but has no relevance in this context (such as personal development and relations) was omitted.

I should have described the evil acts which occurred to millions of victims deported by the Nazis from all over Europe as presented in many books. But how could I have described them along with the emotions accompanying these scenes when I was not there to witness those horrors and emotions?

Later, as an afterthought, I added an Epilogue on our first impressions of Canada; after all, our move there was a consequence of our wartime and postwar experiences. I also included Appendices containing a couple of short studies on ideas that occupied me at various times as I was working on the main text.

Two observations motivated me to write my story. The first came while reading some of the published personal accounts describing the same period. Most of these were written by prominent people who by personality and temperament were more aggressive, more assertive, and on occasion more provocative than we lesser creatures would have been under similar circumstances. Many were true heroes, taking enormous risks; no wonder they had gotten into some hair-raising situations, the accounts of which then made for exciting reading. In contrast, the situations described in my narrative were largely forced upon us, ordinary people, without any provocation on our part. We seemed to be "antiheroes": our attitude was generally passive, unwilling to take large risks—we were lacking the virtues of a traditional hero. We were ordinary people exposed to extraordinary events that we could not deal with, not to mention, control. Yet, these were the attitudes of most people I knew, a story much less often documented. I wanted to show the immense dangers and stresses to which even people like us were exposed during those vicious years—if some of us survived the Nazi times, it was most often due to sheer luck.

The second observation was that, to my surprise, most people we met after our arrival in Canada in 1957, including colleagues at work, somehow assumed that we were born the day we entered the country. We were never asked about details of our earlier lives or of our escape from Hungary. This was no big deal, but we were surprised: how could we hope to develop meaningful friendships if our backgrounds were never discussed? The discreet behavior of our colleagues could perhaps be explained by the general Canadian attitude of not wanting to dig into anyone's past (a reticence alien to most of us with a European background) or by the assumption that since we were very young then, nothing of great significance had likely happened in our lives before. However, we had eventful lives before our "births"—this should be clear from the following chapters. In fact, during our early years we lived through far more extraordinary situations (some bad, even evil) than during the fifty or so years that have passed since we settled in Canada.

Actually, while working on the text, I realized that there was a third reason to write down these stories. The ranks of those who are older than I am are fast thinning out, and those among them who can still remember details of the early days are becoming members of an endangered species. People younger than I, even by only two or three years, don't remember many of the events—they were still children during the war years. So, I realized that it was a duty to write down my stories before they, and the atmosphere and moods they evoke, are becoming lost forever. Unfortunately, I cannot promise and not even hope that documenting and preserving details of those times of terror and horror would prevent such times from ever occurring again: the elimination of future oppressors and vicious wars seems to be an idle dream. But perhaps one can help in extending the more or less civilized period before the next eruption of a global catastrophe.

As I was composing the text, I found that even my memory was on several occasions quite fallible, mostly about sequences—what happened first and what happened later. I was greatly helped by my diaries (logbooks, really) that I have kept since 1940. But these logbooks contained only a very coarse framework of daily events. I had recorded no details and no emotions, good or painful. I had to flesh out the frames from memory (it is amazing how details can return after some prompting), with comments freely added. For some of these comments, I leaned on a few books in my library containing much factual information on the period, and on the recollections of several friends. I trust that nowhere did I cross the line into fiction—that would have been contrary to the mandate I set for myself.

Concerning the manner of presentation, I realized not long after I completed the first few pages that I unwittingly settled on a form where an older self of me appears to be narrating stories about my younger self who is the protagonist of the stories. This enables the narrator to make all kinds of comments and provide insights, often by referring to events that were occur later and were clearly not known at the time of the actual happenings. This approach contrasts with the form of presentation where the protagonist would, as it were, make entries in a diary at the end of every day, and these entries, strung together, would constitute the story. Many successful memoirs have been written in this style. My choice was instinctive, not premeditated, and I have felt comfortable with it during the entire period of writing.

I am grateful to Professor Bruce Bowden of Trinity College, University of Toronto, for selecting a draft of the first two parts as a reading material for several classes, then organizing sessions where this and other books on the war and postwar years were discussed, and asking the classes to write short essays on their impressions. I had the opportunity to read some of the essays and was amazed at the perceptivity, depth, and sensitivity of these studies by young people who, after all, were born decades after the events in my stories had occurred, and in a strange country, thousands of miles away from where most of them were raised. Reading these essays about my work was an unusual and most rewarding experience.

Toronto, December 2008   J. E.

Acknowledgements

While working on the text, I have received many comments from friends whom I gave early drafts; I wanted to see whether they find my chapters interesting or boring. Many were encouraging, some were not. Nevertheless, I am grateful to all because I learned so much from the remarks, both approving and critical.

I am most indebted to those friends who went through the text in great detail, providing many good comments and suggesting excellent changes. This group includes, in alphabetical order, Barbara Brown, Anna Gray, Lesley Kelley-Regnier, John Lorinc, and Andrea Retfalvi. Also, many thanks to my wonderful editors at iUniverse who went into minute details to make my text sound better; most of their suggestions I was only too happy to accept. I am also greatly indebted to Prof. István Deák of Columbia University, New York City, for reading the entire manuscript and pointing out a number of inaccuracies which I could then correct.

Finally, two who deserve special mention—both appear frequently in my stories. One is Andrew Elek, close friend since the darkest days in 1944, with whom we have regularly rediscovered the changing world around us, and discussed its weirdness in many an argument, some lasting until his early death in 2012. The other is—last but not least—my wife Edit, to whom I am most grateful for her unfailing support, encouragement, and numerous comments resulting in many improvements in my narrative.

Part 1

THE NAZI YEARS

Childhood

I was born into an unruly world. Germany, Austria, and Hungary, having lost the 1914–1918 war and having been forced to accept draconian settlements, saw their economies crumble; their politics, too, showed signs of instability. The new Soviet Union to the east, with its openly expansionist policies, frightened most people (Bolsheviks were often rumored to be eating children for breakfast), while they did not know what to make of Mussolini and his Fascist regime in Italy. Nazi Germany was not yet in existence, and until it came in 1933, people did not believe it ever would.

Hungary, the country of my birth, had the dubious distinction of having the first ultra-nationalist totalitarian regime in central Europe. After a couple of very turbulent years following the war, a new army, including nationalist and racist terror gangs called "Officers' Detachments," took over the country in 1920. The army was led by Rear Admiral Miklós Horthy, a former aide in the court of Habsburg Emperor Francis Joseph and, later, commander of the Austro-Hungarian Navy. The detachments initially entertained themselves by randomly beating up and often killing Jews and also others. The new system also produced the first anti-Semitic law in the region, the *numerus clausus*, that regulated the number of Jews admissible to universities or as members of professions. Later, things became more civilized and the dictatorship less forceful; but under the new banner of Christian Hungary, Jews and other "aliens" were made to feel unwelcome. "Jewish" stood for decadent, something contrary to Christian morality. Mussolini, arriving on the scene in Italy in 1922, greatly admired Horthy.

Hungary was now a kingdom without a king. Admiral Horthy became the head of state as a regent. By all appearances, middle-class life was comfortable again by 1927, the year of my birth. Yet, amidst the outwardly gracious living, the prevailing political atmosphere was greatly disturbing. Many felt the need to provide their families with greater security. The violent days of 1920 prompted many well-known scientists and artists of Jewish origin to flee the country. Others, like my maternal grandfather, a prominent doctor, felt it necessary to convert from Judaism to the Roman Catholic faith (although faith had very little to do with it). Like many, he thought this would protect the family from whatever anti-Semitic violence the future would bring—in hindsight, this was a well-intended but very naïve assumption. All his children followed suit, yet my grandmother, a highly independent woman, refused to convert (as a result, my grandparents are buried in different cemeteries).

In contrast, my father came from a modest, lower-middle-class family, which did not feel the same pressures or the same need to blend in with the Magyar[1] society. Consequently, they remained Jewish, for better or for worse. When my parents married, they agreed that all their children would become Roman Catholics, an arrangement (called *reverzális*) which was quite widespread at the time.

So there was I, the first Christian born member of the family. My parents, however, had little experience in Christian parenting. While they thought they did all that was required to properly bring up a little Catholic boy, they forgot about a most important step, namely, that he must be baptized before being accepted into the Church. When, two

---

1   Originally, there was no difference between the meaning of the words "Magyar" and "Hungarian" (P. Ignotus, *Hungary*, Praeger, New York, 1972). Later, in the twentieth century, the distinction has been adopted that the ethnic or language group is "Magyar," whereas the political state or nation is "Hungarian." This is, however, a soft rule, it has never been applied consistently.

years later, somebody reminded them of this omission, they hurriedly took me to the district parish church where the ceremony was duly performed. Yet, the kind priests were not above punishing us for the oversight. When, in filling out the baptismal certificate, the prelate came to the question of where my parents were married (like most others under similar circumstances, they had only a city-hall wedding, not recognized by the Church), the good man did not leave the line open as it was customary in such cases but entered the not too complimentary answer, "Illegitimate." My parents were not amused. Neither were they years later when I proudly showed this document to anyone in sight (I must have thought, to be illegitimate was a rare distinction).

Otherwise, my preschool years were uneventful. Both my parents were working, which was necessary because, as I learned later, my father could not get his license as a professional engineer for some ten years. During that period, he was reduced to doing some consulting and design work. Jews were discriminated against in many ways, and this became only worse in the late 1930s when the Hungarian government started to take over pages from the German script. But I am getting ahead of myself.

* * *

The next time the realities of the outside world had an impact on me was during my first week at school. School suited me fine; I was not crying for my mother like many of my schoolmates, as I was already used to her absence during the day. On the third day, however, something surprising happened. Our teacher announced that the next class would be religious instruction and we would have to separate into groups of the same religion and attend instruction in different classrooms. The reader must know that in those days church and state were not separated in Hungary, so religious instruction was part of the curriculum and scheduled the same way as any other subject. All the kids got up and went in search of the appointed rooms. All but one—

that was me. I didn't understand a word of it. The teacher, Mrs. Sávoly, was bemused and annoyed to equal degree.

"Why don't you go like all the others?" she inquired.

"I don't know where to go," came my laconic answer.

"What is your religion?" she asked.

"What is religion?" I asked back.

By that time she was no longer bemused, only annoyed. "We will have to look it up in the book." After searching the class roster, she announced, "You are a Roman Catholic, go to room so-and-so and join the others!"

So I went. I found my classmates standing in front of a teacher who was dressed in a brown habit with a white rope tied around his waist, the two ends hanging down—he was a Franciscan friar, I later learned. The children were just practicing how to cross themselves; some looked quite awkward, trying to do it with both hands. I quietly joined the group and soon became an expert in the art.

The whole experience was rather upsetting, though; I thought I should have been prepared for such an eventuality. So that evening, after dinner, I asked my parents for some explanation. They handled the situation beautifully: they sat down with me, took all the time it needed, and explained the whole background in a very frank manner. And a complex bundle it was. I learned about religions, about Jews, and that they were not very popular at the moment. I also found out about my own status: that I had a Roman Catholic mother and a Jewish father and that, at present, such a mixed parentage was not a winning combination. Here I became a bit confused and asked what, in the light of all this, was my religion—the teacher today said I was a Roman Catholic. My parents suggested, with some uncertainty in their voices, that since I was registered at birth as a Roman Catholic, that was my religion and not the Jewish faith (the "Jewish laws" did not exist yet, and my parents stuck to the old way of classifying people by religion and not by origin).

That night, in bed, I considered my options and instinctively rejected the possibility of keeping silent at school about my origins; an elaborate web of lies appeared neither attractive nor practical (I was not a good liar, that much I knew). I felt that people should know me (and like or dislike me) for what I was and not for a false image I would be promoting. All this I could not have articulated then the way I do it here, but the fact is that I have always been quite open about my origins.

As a consequence, at school everybody knew about my unusual situation. Yet nothing unpleasant came out of it. In fact, Father Valér, the monk who was our religion teacher, a very decent, kind, almost saintly person, treated me as the prodigal son who finally returned to the fold; I was among his favorites in the class. That I didn't mind.

Grade one was a glorious year. In a large part, our teacher Mrs. Sávoly was responsible for this. First, it had become a tradition that her class would be an "experimental co-ed class," boys and girls together. This was quite unique in the city, but she made great success of it. For us, it proved to be a most stimulating experience. Second, she had a winning personality: motherly and kind, firm but never harsh. No wonder we all, Sávoly graduates over the years, have kept her memory in special affection. To this day, when we accidentally meet someone who turns out to be an ex-student of the elementary school at Marczibányi Square, the question invariably follows, "Were you also in Mrs. Sávoly's co-ed class?" And if yes, an invisible bond immediately develops, as if we were members of a special order of knights.

* * *

But back to earth! An interesting experience occurred a year later, in grade two. Although the school was pleasant, anti-Semitism was not quite absent; if nowhere else, it existed in the sometimes overblown talk and gestures of the children. It appeared to be fairly harmless. If there were Jews in the class who were loud and obnoxious, it only fed these outbursts. The boy who sat in front of me, Tom S., was such a kid—loud, aggressive, a bully. As a consequence, I joined the anti-Semitic clique and used the same language as they did when we talked about Tom. The mind of a seven-year old apparently did not find any contradiction in this and could accommodate these feelings knowing full well that he, too, was a Jew.[2] My anti-Semitic period was cut short by an adult who asked me to describe exactly why I disliked Jews. To my embarrassment, I could not give an answer, and that was the end of my sojourn on the extreme right.

Another event of interest happened in grade four. One day, during one of the intervals between classes, I stayed in the classroom to work on something important, perhaps a part of my homework. I was alone, the others were playing outside. Suddenly one of my classmates, Anti Engler, rushed in and suggested that I should join the others, they have great fun outside. I politely declined. He left but returned a minute later and repeated his suggestion—this time I told him to get lost. He seemingly did but then returned again and continued pestering me. I felt, enough was enough, stood up and gave him a good slap in the face, whereupon he left, crying. I assumed the story was closed and had no second thoughts about it, until the next Tuesday.

That day, our teacher, Mr. Zsemlye, came in and started the morning with some general matters as he always did. Suddenly, I heard my name in connection with a complaint he received from Engler that, without provocation, I slapped him in his face. Would I please tell my side of the story? I did. Mr. Zsemlye, a man we all liked, told me that it was not my prerogative to judge and punish Engler; I should have reported the case to him, and he would have decided what to do. He sentenced me to stay at school after classes and write it down fifty times that "I should leave judging and punishing people to those whose job it was to do that."

---

2   Throughout this narrative, I am freely employing the increasingly accepted parlance of the time, where anyone is regarded a Jew who is that by law or origin and not just by religion or belief. This essentially racist definition has been widely used in Hungary to this day.

I was confused and angry. Angry because the required procedure run against my early decision never to report or inform on my classmates. I didn't want to become a *spicli,* a "squealer." I did what I was ordered to do but decided to ask for more explanation. So I waited for Mr. Zsemlye and, as we lived in the same building, we walked home together. He gave me a short lesson in democracy: while admitting that "my way" might be faster and more efficient, the "democratic way" he described would be in the long run fairer because it would often protect people from unjust punishments. The price of this "fair" process was that one had to wait a long time before the verdicts were announced; the process was usually quite slow.[3] As we entered our building, I was still not totally convinced—it took me years to fully understand the difference between the two approaches. This was my first lesson in democracy and its complex ways but certainly not the last.

* * *

All in all, the four years in elementary school were fun. I made many friends, Jews and non-Jews alike. Hostility and hatred, either at school or in the outside world, were virtually unknown to me. All this left me completely unprepared for the rough ride which was awaiting me in the *gymnasium,* as the schools offering grades five to twelve were then called. My happy childhood was over at the age of ten.

---

3 Churchill's famous dictum was not yet known: "I prefer an inefficient democracy to an efficient dictatorship."

Dark Clouds Gather

Nineteen thirty seven, the year I entered the gymnasium, already had the foreboding of worse things to come, and I started to become aware of what was going on around me. It happened a year later that the first law about restricting Jews was ratified by the Hungarian Parliament. The document contained a long list of things Jews were no longer allowed to do, mainly by capping the percentage of their membership in professional and other licensing bodies. This was in response to a famous speech by prime minister Darányi early in 1938 who "candidly" recognized that a "Jewish problem" did exist, and defined it as the out-of-proportion participation of Jews in industry, banking, commerce, the arts, and professions such as medicine and law.

Hard on the heels of the first law came the second, in 1939, with further restrictions. However, the most important part of this new law was the definition of who was to be regarded a Jew. We learned that basically anyone with more than one Jewish grandparent was to be considered a Jew. There were exceptions, such as those who were born as Christians if both parents had converted before their child was born or if one parent was Christian and the other converted before 1939—such persons were allowed to have two Jewish grandparents and still didn't count as Jews. If both parents converted before 1919 and, in addition, it could be proven that all ancestors had lived in the country for almost a century, the person would not be regarded a Jew, irrespective of the number of Jewish grandparents. Other exceptions were listed, too, but none applied to my family. The basic definition was harsh and outdid even Hitler's definition of who was a Jew, as laid down in the infamous Nuremberg laws.

I clearly recall having been fully aware of both laws and also remember the scenes where the three of us, my parents and I, were intently listening to the radio broadcasting news of the parliamentary debates and the final announcement of these monstrous documents. Needless to say, these were not cheerful moments; my father listening tight-lipped and mother at times noticeably trembling.

In 1941, a third law about Jews was ratified, forbidding marriage and even sex between Jews and Christians. Considering my degree of maturity at not quite fourteen, this law did not upset me quite as much as the previous one.

* * *

As I found out soon enough, the atmosphere at the gymnasium was accurately responding to the spirit of times and was overflowing with nationalism and anti-Semitism. My classmates were the sons of medium- or high-ranking bureaucrats in the nearby government departments, or of janitors, barbers, butchers, and other tradesmen living in the area. Both groups had a vested interest in being loyal to the government of the day, and since the government was nationalistic and anti-Semitic, so were they, with great enthusiasm. Sons of the former group were politely anti-Semitic, sons of the latter were rude and often violent.

And, then, there were the teachers! Many were sadistic or anti-Semitic or both. Take our professor of botany, Dr. Tokody. A fat, balding man with an ugly, pockmarked face, he was misanthropic in general but liked the Jews the least. In the first fifteen minutes of the class, we had to report on our homework. The general routine, used by almost all teachers, was that we were called to the blackboard at random, after they flipped back and forth through the pages of their small notebooks with the list of names. We were desperately trying to guess whether the names on the page just open were at the beginning, middle, or end of the alphabet—some teachers deliberately made this into a cruel game. Tokody would do the page-turning exercise and suddenly call out, "Idiot!" We didn't know what to do. He repeated, "Idiot!" until the boy with the weakest nerves slowly got up. "Not this idiot, the other one!" shouted Tokody, and took his time to repeat the process until the boy he wanted finally stood up. By that time the poor guy was completely destroyed and could only make inarticulate noises in response to Tokody's questions on his homework. "Well, my son," Tokody leaned back with a broad gesture, "where were you yesterday, at home to prepare for today's classes, or at the Ganz factory where they pummeled your head with a steam-hammer?" The guy pulled himself together as much as he could, and in a shaky voice assured Tokody that he was at home, studying. No one ever dared to choose the factory option, we were too young. "So, why can't you answer my questions?"—and the poor fellow was dismissed, with a failing mark entered. Tokody had a variety of ways to torture his victims, and Jews were the first in line for the treatment. Rumor had it that he was also corrupt.

Or consider Mr. Girschik, teacher of mathematics. Luckily, we saw him only rarely, when he substituted for one of our regular teachers. He would not use his notebook, just point to the fellow he wanted to examine. But if it was a Jew, he would walk up to the guy and pull him up by his almost non-existent sideburns, which in Girschik's mind represented the side curls Orthodox Jews grow at that place. I can tell the reader that this exercise was extremely painful.

Or the Roman Catholic priest, the Reverend Petró, a bright but vicious person, who taught us that everyone outside the Church was doomed, the Jews in the first place. When we were fifteen, he took it on himself to provide us with sex education, for which he was obviously well qualified. He warned us against the sinful and unhealthy practice of self-gratification (an obsession of his; he used the ominous-sounding term "self-infection") and even thinking of sex before marriage. Instead, we should emulate St. Emery, the son of the first Christian king of Hungary, who died in a hunting accident almost a thousand years ago, aged thirty, and allegedly still a virgin. Here, the Reverend suddenly turned to me, "Endrényi, will you wipe that sarcastic Jewish smirk off your face?[4]" I was not the only one reacting with a smirk, but only I had a Jewish one.

Our teacher of physical education, Mr. Sykó, disliked the Jews only because most of them were not very athletic. But he was a sadist. He would punish those who chatted during his explanations by calling both transgressors to the blackboard and ordering them to slap each other in the face. If the hits were not as strong as he wanted (which was likely under the circumstances), he would go and demonstrate it himself. He was a strong man.

In all fairness I must add that not every teacher was as unbearable as those mentioned. Some provided just the kind of relief we needed to endure our days at school. One of these was Dénes Lengyel, our homeroom teacher for three years. He did everything he could to protect us from abuses. Still in his twenties, Dr. Lengyel's teaching methods were unconventional, more like friendly chats, during which he learned to know us well enough that he never had to ask for formal accounts of our homework. He was handicapped by the fact that he himself was of partly Jewish origin; from 1943 on, I found out later, he went through hard times in forced labor camps and then in Soviet captivity (this could happen to Jews as well). From his memoirs published in 2007, twenty years after his death, he emerges as a person who always tried to act true to his principles, values formed during his upbringing in a family of prominent writers and teachers. During a visit with him in 1985, I was amazed to find that he considered the *Toldy* of those years an even worse place than I did and gave a most unflattering description of the school in his memoirs.

---

4   For "face" he used the word *pofa*—a rude equivalent.

Another teacher on whom I could rely emotionally was Dr. Károly Kresznerics, professor of mathematics and our homeroom teacher for the remaining years. An almost foolishly fearless person who made no secret of his distaste for the Nazis, he stood up for us on numerous occasions. He died in January, 1945, during the brutal siege of Buda, from a heart attack. Since he had no children, these lines are meant to serve as a lone memorial for a magnificent person, a truly humane individual.

Most boys in the class were as cruel as teenagers could be. While I don't remember major incidents, verbal abuse was frequent; I must admit that, as a converted Jew, I received somewhat less than my fair share of it. But there was plenty of "polite" discrimination of which the following incident is a good example. At the age of eleven or twelve, we formed little clubs in the class, each with some important but highly secret mission; I became a member of one. One day, the president of my club, Laci Zay, informed me that to his great regret it was decided that Jews could no longer belong to the club. I wasn't too upset, but the memory of the incident has still clung to me over the years. (After a long hiatus, Zay and I became good friends in the 80s and 90s and our friendship lasted until his death in 2000.) The Jewish students were a small minority in the class, about 10 percent, and we didn't make friends across the line; we tended to become loners.

* * *

Not every gymnasium in the city was as bad as ours. In many, at least in the central districts, the atmosphere was more congenial, partly due to the fact that the proportion of Jews was higher and thus they were in a better position to assert themselves. Just a block away from our school was the *Mátyás*, rumored to be a more pleasant place than our *Toldy*. Actually, it wasn't so great either. My life-long friend, Péter Sándor, who was a student at *Mátyás*, never failed to remind me of the inferior education I received at such an intellectually dilapidated, Nazi-infested place as the *Toldy*. The questions of course arise, why my parents enrolled me in the *Toldy* in the first place and, given this, why did I not change schools later? The answer to the first question may be that the school possibly had a good reputation from earlier times; the answer to the second had its roots in my inertia, which made me slow to accept changes (even if they would have been for the better), and in the surprisingly little help I received from my parents—perhaps they were not aware of the extent of the problem.

At about this time, an incident rudely reminded me that ugly events could occur anywhere, not only at school. One day I was walking home from my piano lesson, fully absorbed in my thoughts as always when, suddenly, two little guys blocked my way. They could have been a year or two younger than I was, but were already threatening and noisy hooligans. "Are you a Jew?" they demanded to know. I hesitantly admitted it. A brawl ensued, interspersed with the use of some foul language. The scene ended only when I threatened to call the police, the prospect of which they didn't consider attractive and decided to run away.

The incident, however, greatly upset me. I arrived home in tears and my parents, not used to such emotional displays on my part, didn't quite know what to do with me. They tried to point out that these things were often happening to others, too, and at my age I would be perhaps oversensitive, but they couldn't calm me down. I myself could not explain what was disturbing me so much. Today, I think, I understand it better: while I programmed myself to absorb unpleasantness at school, I considered all other times, including those spent on the street, my own and was greatly disturbed by this invasion of my privacy—my freedom. Was I, after this experience, to spend all my time when walking on the streets by looking out for possible attackers? This prospect highly depressed me; I couldn't handle it, and it took me several months to regain my balance. And, of course, I didn't know that life constantly interferes with one's privacy, even at much better times.

* * *

The Second World War started on September 1, 1939. I vividly remember the headlines of the evening papers—I first saw one on a streetcar as someone studied the first page with a very concerned expression on his face—"THE WAR HAS BROKEN OUT" it read in letters larger than I ever had seen before. I had heard much about the horrors of the First World War, but in my mind these stories were as remote as folk tales, never to occur again (as folk tales never do)—and yet, here we were again! Could it be that I would experience similar horrors, would learn first-hand what a war was? I did not know, and could not imagine, that what my generation was to experience during the coming war would easily outdo the horrors of the previous one.

Initially, Hungary stayed neutral. But in 1941, a sequence of events changed this relative calm. In April, German army units crossed Hungarian territory to attack Yugoslavia (this invasion was quite visible in Budapest, and I remember it very well: rows and rows of armored carriers and swank BMW motorcycles), and Hungarian units joined in without the consent of the prime minister, Count Pál Teleki. The fact that the Hungarian government only three months earlier had signed an eternal friendship pact with Yugoslavia was simply ignored. Teleki considered these events such a serious breach of his word and stain on his honor that he shot himself. A new government was installed that was far more inclined to cooperate with the Germans. When Germany attacked the Soviet Union in June, the Hungarian government, reacting to a false provocation, declared war on the Soviets without delay. First trying to postpone action, Britain declared war on Hungary in December; and after Pearl Harbor (also in December), Hungary, following the Germans, immediately joined the war against the United States. By the end of the year, Hungary found herself at war with some formidable enemies.

After June, war measures in the cities were hurriedly introduced. Windows were darkened, car headlights were dimmed, even the light on my bicycle received a contraption to prevent the enemy from finding out where I was. Air-raid shelters were built, and we practiced putting on and taking off gas masks, things we never actually used during the war. A formidable mess was caused by converting the left-hand drive system, prevailing until then, to the right-hand system, for the convenience of German "visitors."

At school, special military exercises were introduced, once a week for three hours. They were called *levente*-trainings, the ancient word *levente* meaning a young fighter. Not being a very athletic type, I hated these exercises, with one exception: I enjoyed target-shooting, mainly because I was good at it. But within a few months, an edict was handed down that Jews could no longer participate in the *levente*-training, partly because their presence would pollute the Christian morality of the young fighters and partly because Jews were not to handle guns. However, since Jews were not to be let off the hook so easily, they had to form special auxiliary units that, for three hours a week, were to do all kinds of menial tasks.

That didn't sound good, and it wasn't. We all had to report to the district *levente* center at an appointed hour, and as we lined up to receive instructions, I noticed that Jews from all gymnasiums in the district were present. We didn't wait long before our new commander showed up: an army colonel. At first it was surprising that such a high-ranking officer would be assigned to perform such a lowly task as commanding Jewish teenagers to do cleanup chores, but soon we found out the reason: the colonel was continually drunk and even this job was somewhat over his head.

The great man first made a speech to us—this became a regular opening number at these get-togethers. He would stand on a balcony above us and from this imposing pulpit he would lecture us. "Filthy Jews!"[5]—this was our standard address. He then explained all the things he would not tolerate, too numerous to list here. Thereupon we

---

5   *Büdös zsidók!*—literally "stinking Jews." A rather frequently used epithet those days, none too kind.

were divided into small groups, each issued a wheelbarrow and some brooms, and ordered to clean up all the streets in the vicinity. Since horse-drawn carts were still quite common, our job included cleaning up after the horses (without gloves, of course). Our enthusiasm for the task was moderate. Other weeks, after the introductory address, we had to haul important objects to important places or wash the windows of the center. And so it went; our ingenious colonel managed to find something for us every Thursday.

Of the colonel's remarkable speeches, one in particular has stuck in my memory. "Filthy Jews," he roared, "I find you such a disgusting bunch that there is no doubt if I looked out of some window and you showed your naked asses in the next, nobody could tell the difference!" We froze. Obviously, he was so drunk that he reversed the metaphor. "What! Are you not ashamed of yourselves?" And he repeated his version. Then somebody couldn't hold it in any longer and burst into a high-pitched, uncontrolled laughter. Others followed, and soon the entire group lost all control and jumped up and down, laughing hysterically, not caring about the consequences. For a moment, the colonel was caught by surprise. Then, with a somewhat uncertain gait, he descended from his balcony and started to beat us at random with his cane. We tried to scatter to avoid being hit, some with more success than others. It was amazing how long he could go on, considering his condition.

We all hated these afternoons, and I was always quite depressed the mornings before. Our parents listened to our accounts of these exercises with horror and disbelief. At this point we, the kids, had far more experience in being discriminated against and roughed up and humiliated than our parents who still lived (most of them, anyway) in acceptable and uninterrupted comfort. Admittedly, in a minority of Jewish families tragedy struck early. Late in 1941, several Jewish auxiliary labor units accompanied the regular army into the Ukraine and beyond. Like the army, they were not prepared for the harsh Russian winter and many died, partly from exposure, partly from illness, and partly from the cruelty of their guards.[6] My future wife's father was one of these, a victim of typhoid fever.

In time, our weekly exercises became less trying. Sometimes there was nothing to do. At other times, we were ordered to report to the district fire brigade for training; there we learned how to run hoses, how to join them, and how to open fire hydrants. This work was better, I must admit, than being exposed to the colonel.

Dr. Kresznerics, our homeroom teacher, somehow learned about these conditions. Early in 1943, he came upon the brilliant idea that a few of us could be dispensed from our obligations to serve the colonel and, instead, assigned to him to help cleaning up and reorganizing the teachers' library at the school. Amazingly, his idea was accepted and we (I was one of the lucky ones chosen) began our new life dusting books and trying to arrange them into some order, for three hours every week. I cannot describe the relief I felt. Since the library was in a poor shape, our activity went on for more than a year.

* * *

In Hungary, the second part of 1942 and all of 1943 represented an unusual lull in wartime activities. A new government led by Miklós Kállay took over, which was less convinced about the merits of taking part in the war and tried to find a way to survive until the end with a minimum of war effort. A second goal of the government was to gain enough goodwill among the Allied leaders to ensure a decent settlement for Hungary after the war (and the survival of the government). Secret deals were arranged with the Allies, with the result that the latter did not bomb Hungarian cities during that period. Life went on as if there was no war: people were busy, streetcars and buses were running, daily performances sold out at the theatres. While the Jews did not know

---

6   A blood-chilling scene of guards cruelly murdering a Jew from a labor unit is shown in the 1999 film *Sunshine*. The sequence depicted could not have been invented; it must have been based on extensive interviews. See also: *Swimming Across*, Andrew S. Grove, Warner Books, 2001, p. 169.

anything about the deals, they clung to the hope that in this more civilized atmosphere they just might sail unharmed into the post-Hitler world. But how could the government (or the Jews) believe that the Germans would not notice anything?

In the meantime, the fortunes of war that had favored the Germans and their allies until then, started to turn around. A major contribution to this change occurred late in 1942, when the Soviet Army stopped the advance of the Germans at Stalingrad (today, Volgograd) and forced them into retreat, a retreat that continued until the war's end. The German war communiqués became obscure, reporting daily on military regroupings and planned evacuations, desperately trying to mask the facts. For us, however, it was important to learn the truth about the war events; our hopes depended on it. As a result, most of us became addicted to the daily ritual of tuning in to London, which we could receive on the shortwave band. The reception was sometimes clear, at other times heavily jammed. To this day, I can hear the voice of the announcer: "*Itt London beszél ...* This is London calling. We are broadcasting the Hungarian-language news of the British Radio." It was exciting, but also completely illegal. We had to make sure that the apartment was locked and all curtains were drawn in the room where the radio was. Even so, our classmates constantly heckled us about listening to the London broadcasts (and some teachers, too, like that clown Rezik, our music teacher) that at times, when strangers were present, could have been quite dangerous.

During the Kállay period, things didn't get worse for the Jews, but they didn't get much better either. More and more people were drafted into the auxiliary labor units, and although now they were not taken out of the country, they had easy or miserable times depending on their work and the attitude of the guards. At home, my mother had to leave her job because, as a Jew, she no longer could be trusted. I was not enjoying school more than before, but now school life went hand-in-hand with the more usual activities of a sixteen-year-old: going to concerts, attending parties, learning to dance, even dating. Then, back to school every morning—it was almost a double life.

Life was not the same as before even at the place where I spent my summer holidays. This was an attractive lodge called *Lepence*, operated by one of my uncles and situated at a beautiful spot on the Danube, near the village of Visegrád. I loved to be there; life at the lodge was in a complete contrast to the dreariness of school and the other things I hated during the winter. Nevertheless, we had to put up with an increasing number of restrictions. The province where the lodge was located had a particularly vicious governor (the infamous László Endre, hanged after the war for his Nazi activities). In 1942, he ordered the confiscation of all radios in Jewish hands, including the one at the lodge. This left us without news and music for that summer and the next. In 1943, our last summer there, the governor decreed that Jews were not allowed to swim in the rivers of his province. So we had to row over to the other side of the Danube (this was not disallowed), and since the other side was in another province, we could safely swim there. Or we could ride our bicycles three kilometers to the next village, which happened to be located in a third province, and swim there on "our" side of the river. We did all of these without feeling much restricted because we, teenagers, learned to adapt quickly to almost anything. But, in retrospect, these limitations provided a foretaste of further restrictions that were soon to follow, and had we recognized this, we would have been rather frightened instead of feeling so easygoing.

One of the almost surreal events at the lodge in 1943 was that, while we (mostly of Jewish origin) were happily vacationing there, a Jewish forced labor unit was stationed in the back garden for a few weeks. We felt we had to act in a brotherly fashion and took food and books to them. They were grateful, and we felt smug—but also guilty about the whole situation of forced inequality that was essentially humiliating to them. It was a bizarre situation that we didn't want but had no control over.

The Storm Moves in

The relative peace in Hungary ended abruptly in March 1944. In its successful thrust to the west, the Soviet Army was about to enter Hungarian territory and the Germans needed full control over the area. They were aware of Kállay's game and had to put an end to it.

March 19 was a beautiful, sunny, warm Sunday. Windows were open all over the city, and the air was full with the fragrance of early spring, smells coming from the hills surrounding Buda. We were having our leisurely Sunday breakfast when the phone rang. It was an aunt of mine who in great excitement informed us that the Germans had occupied the city. She was living on one of the main boulevards and could see from her window what was happening. In her excitement, my aunt announced the news in English, a foolish step considering that, after all, it was the enemy's language and such communication could be suspicious. For an hour, my father was beside himself on that account alone. But then he realized, as we all knew instinctively, what the main significance of the news was: the day represented the beginning of a new and dark era in our lives, the ending of which was completely unpredictable for all of us.

By noon, the radio stopped broadcasting its regular program and aired martial music instead. In the news that followed some time later, the protective occupation of Hungary by the German forces was announced, and that Kállay and his cabinet had been replaced by a new cabinet led by Döme Sztójay, former ambassador to Berlin and a known stooge of the Germans. Later that afternoon, rumors reached us (mostly on the phone, shrouded in very careful language) that many prominent people in the city, mainly Jews but also non-Jews, had been arrested by the Germans and taken to their headquarters. The Germans moved at an incredible speed; we did not have much sleep that night.

School went ahead the next morning as if nothing had happened. Our teachers tried to ignore external events as much as possible; this seemed to be a fundamental attitude in our school. In 1979, thirty-five years after the war, an anniversary publication of the school still managed to ignore the war and its effects, except for mentioning that the school building was heavily damaged. It proudly reported that absences without justification during 1944 were on the decrease when compared to earlier years (if one didn't count the absences of those who were killed—or these absences were considered justified).

In the following days, new orders by the Germans were posted almost hourly. Schools were ordered to terminate the spring term by April 5, making teachers scramble to select the most important material for the remaining two weeks. Jews were forbidden to travel by trains. Even their travel within the cities was restricted. But the most devastating decree was that, beginning on April 5, all Jews had to wear a yellow star on their coats or shirts in public places. The color, size, and method of affixing the star were precisely described. Penalties for not complying were severe. We read the news with great agitation; it was the first indication that we were no longer considered human beings, only marked animals.

* * *

On the afternoon of the fourth, my mother was diligently sewing the stars onto our overcoats. Very little was said; we were all numb emotionally—we knew the implications but didn't want to think of them, let alone talk about them. What was happening was utterly incredible. Our usual way of life was destroyed, and from now on, we could look forward to nothing but darkness.

For several families, the experience was even worse. Until then, some parents had decided to protect their children by never telling them about their Jewish origins. That afternoon, they were forced to disclose these secrets and tell them that, from the next day on, they would have to wear the star. In a few minutes, their identities were destroyed and they had to see themselves, and introduce themselves to others, as completely different (and apparently undesirable) persons.

The next day was the last day of school, with the usual closing ceremonies. It was to start with a thanksgiving mass at church (to express our thanks for all the good things that happened to us during the year) and continue at the school where, after some speeches, the report cards would be distributed. My parents saw unknown dangers in everything (not quite unreasonably) and were dead set against my attending the mass, but my mind was made up and I insisted on going. I wanted to test the waters. So, against their wish, I got up early and left the house shortly after seven in the morning, with my brand-new star neatly fixed on my overcoat.

At that hour, only a few people were on the street. The first person to walk in the opposite direction, a man, noticed my star from some distance and, as he hurried by me, he looked the other way in obvious embarrassment. I must have been the first starred person he met. This performance was repeated a few more times. And then, in the distance, I noticed a figure with a star approaching.

It turned out to be a girl, about my age. She was a stranger, I had never seen her before. As we got close, our eyes met for a split second. It was a moment I'll never forget. There was something in the expression of her eyes, encouragement, assurance, as if she would say, "Cheer up, we will survive!"—and she was gone. Goethe must have been inspired by such an experience when he wrote, "The eternal feminine leads us on."

I turned into a side street and soon reached the square in front of the church, where we had to meet. From a distance, I could already see my classmates and wondered about the reception I would get. They would be rude as always, I guessed, and tease me about my new decoration, ask me how much I paid for it, and the like. I wasn't exactly looking forward to this experience. But as I joined the group, the only one with a star, something remarkable happened. In a subdued manner, the boys came up to me, one by one, and shook my hand. I was moved to tears.

Much later, I started to understand. These were boys, after all, not adults. They were playing games with us, at times cruel games, but these were *their* games; they had full control over them. And now they realized that their toy had been taken away from them and turned into something serious, even deadly. They never wished on us serious consequences; all they wanted to see was their Jewish classmates squirm and whimper. A few would perhaps turn into real monsters in three or four years' time, but at this stage they were still children. With their handshake, they distanced themselves from the adult game that was as sinister and ominous to them as it was to us.

The time came to enter the church. I felt strange, with my yellow mark that made me stand out in the crowd. The Reverend Petró gave the sermon: he listed all the reasons why we should be thankful on this joyous occasion—did he not notice my star? With the mass over, we marched up to the school, where many of the other Jews joined us. Dr. Kresznerics distributed the booklets containing our year-end marks; he did not make a speech, for which I was grateful. In other years, it was a matter of great excitement to look into the book and find out our standings; this year I hardly looked—it didn't seem to matter any longer.

I left school alone and took a small detour before going home. I went down to the Danube and walked along its tree-lined embankment. How I used to love this place! I walked by the Calvinist church, then past a Roman Catholic church on a square with a large covered market at the far end. Suddenly, a strange thought came to my mind and stopped me in my tracks: could it be that the thanksgiving mass this morning was the last mass I would ever attend? Because, I reasoned, for the next year or so I would be kept busy with other things and, should I not survive the year, I would be right by default. If I survived, I would be (hopefully) entering a world where no one would force me to go to masses, and I promised myself, right then and there, that in that case I would never again attend a Roman Catholic mass. Today, more than sixty years later, I can truthfully say that so far I have kept this promise.

In my resolution to avoid masses, I have been helped by my growing aversion to religions, a view that I had gradually developed since about the age of ten. By sixteen, I found it hard to accept any religious teaching or concept. My particular dislike of the Roman Catholic Church was the result of meeting, or hearing about, people like the Reverend Petró and a few other Fascist priests, some quite famous, some infamous (a few were even armed); also, I could not forget the cozy relation the Church had had with all the right-wing governments under Horthy. There was not much love lost between us.

After this lengthy discussion with myself, I hurried home before my parents could get worried about me. Indeed, they were waiting for me quite anxiously, and I had to give them a detailed account of my day. We discussed everything except my report card, which was forgotten by all of us. My parents were satisfied that it was possible to leave the house with a yellow star and return home safely. At least, for the time being.

* * *

Our lives went on, branded as we were with the yellow star. We got used to it, just as we got used to a score of other restrictions. The Germans and their Hungarian puppets made sure that life would never get boring. During April and May, they ordered us to perform a number of chores. The first I remember was that we had to turn in our radio. So I had to carry the big cabinet to a collection point, where they unceremoniously threw it on a pile of similar big boxes. Next,

I had to hand in my beloved bicycle; Jews were not allowed to own any vehicle. This was a slow affair; they laboriously wrote down the make and year of the bicycle and its serial number. Then, they issued a receipt, indicating all this information. They made it look as if they only wanted to borrow the thing and intended to return it at a later time to the holder of the receipt.

A new aspect in our lives was that we had to endure numerous air raids, often with bombing, that caused heavy damages. Each time, we went to the air-raid shelter and, in the beginning, we were really scared, especially when we heard detonations. Later, our other problems received priority over the air raids; we started to realize that we were more likely to die as a consequence of being Jews than from a bomb hitting our house. I also spent a lot of time, particularly at nights, on duty as an air-raid guard, alerting people when the radio at the neighbors signaled alarm conditions, and supervising the orderly move in and out of the shelter. The old and the new had a curious mix in my life. Before March, I tutored several boys from the school who were behind with their studies; this business, and my income from it, continued well into this period.

In the meantime, we had heard rumors that a systematic roundup of Jews in the provinces was under way and that they would be deported by train to unknown locations. This news was bad enough, but it was made worse by the realization that our turn could not be far away either. We did not know about death camps and gas chambers, and thought mostly that the Jews from the provinces were being deported to Germany to work in some important war industry, as ultimately we, too, would be. Yet, we all instinctively knew that it would be better if we could stay in our own country.

Neither did we know about the cruelty with which the deportations were being carried out. Much later we learned that both Edmund Veesenmayer, the German ambassador to Hungary, and Adolf Eichmann, the infamous executor of Jewish deportations throughout Europe, credited the perfect cooperation of the Hungarian Nazis for the efficiency of the operation. Both were amazed at how helpful the Hungarians were, and stated that they had never experienced such willingness to assist them in any other country. It is one of the darkest pages in Hungarian history.

For the time being, there were no organized deportations from Budapest. We heard that people were arrested, seemingly at random, but at first we didn't know personally anyone who was taken away. So it felt like a rude awakening when, around the middle of May, Mió, my girlfriend, and her mother were picked up at home and interned to the former Rabbinical School, a clearinghouse for people to be deported. I dearly wished I could help but didn't know how. I had no real or magic powers. Finally, I made a phone call to a prominent person whose name was suggested to me by an uncle of mine, a doctor with a network of useful people. The prominent man was very polite and promised to look into the matter; yet, after a moment of relief, I felt the call was useless: making polite promises was the obvious way of fast getting rid of unwanted callers. Twenty days later, her father managed to free Mió with a much more effective device: a sizeable bribe.

At the end of May, further instructions concerning Jews were posted. One of these ordered every male between the ages of eighteen and forty-eight to report for permanent labor service. This meant that they would be taken to places inside or outside Hungary to do hard physical labor which, as it turned out, they often did not survive. On the last day before they had to leave, I (at sixteen still exempt) visited a few friends, including Péter Sándor, to wish them well. The mood, of course, was terrible, not much encouragement could be offered. Yet, what fate had in store for this family exceeded our imagination: as I said good-bye to Péter and shook hands with his parents, we didn't know that neither I nor Péter would ever see them again.

Shortly after, all Jews were ordered to move to buildings designated as "Jewish houses" by mid-June. The addresses were listed in the announcement, and a yellow star had to be placed over their entrances (see the first cover photo). Our building where we lived was not included, so we had to find a place and move at short notice. Luckily, one of my aunts lived in a designated building, and since she had an extra room, she agreed to accommodate us. It was in her best interest, too, because by a system of quotas she would have had to take in people anyway. So we moved, taking along the most important necessities only—furniture, rugs, paintings, and books were out of the question. On top of it all, fairly restrictive hours when we were allowed to leave the building were imposed.

At the time, we didn't know how close we were to being deported. The Germans planned this for early July, as the last step in eliminating all Jews in Hungary. It was, amazingly enough, Horthy himself who stopped the action. By that time, he and his close circle of advisors were convinced that the war was lost for the Germans, so he became more receptive to the tremendous pressure put on him by countries and states, such as Sweden and the Vatican, and also by the Allied powers themselves, to save at least the Jews in Budapest. He read the hastily assembled notes of two Slovak prisoners who managed to escape from Auschwitz, and thus became aware of the gas chambers and crematoria and their use for mass killing. Also, he was warned of a coup planned against him by members of his own cabinet. Finally, he decided to act. While the Germans worked on the last details and their Hungarian friends put several well-armed units of gendarmes into key positions, Horthy called in military units loyal to him and warned that they would shoot if the Germans went ahead with the deportation. At the last minute, the Germans backed off.

Could we now say that Horthy saved our lives, and we therefore ought to be grateful to him? The reply lies, perhaps, in a joke from a much later period:

"What is the most important task of Socialism?"

"To rectify all the problems which would not have arisen had Socialism not been introduced."

It is a fact that after the war Horthy was never charged, partly because a handwritten letter of protection signed by none other than

Stalin. Horthy was allowed to live out his remaining years peacefully in Portugal.

* * *

Meanwhile, life in our new home was a mix of dodging the ever-increasing number of official edicts and socializing with my cousins and new friends who lived in the same building. Sometimes we had visitors; among them was Andrew Elek, whom I first met under these bleak circumstances, but with whom a life-long friendship ensued. His visits were also eagerly anticipated by all the parents, for a very particular reason. Since Andrew's grandfather was the Chairman of the Jewish Council and an important player in many of the negotiations about the fate of the Jews in the city, the parents would mercilessly quiz Andrew for some confidential information every time they saw him. On one occasion, an aunt of mine begged him on her knees for some news. But each time, he remained loyal to his grandfather's wishes and never divulged anything that was not already generally known.

Interestingly, years later, Andrew became quite critical of his grandfather's policies. He came to believing that the Jews in Budapest should have been warned about all impending dangers, including deportation to death camps, as this would have motivated them to take protective measures, such as going into hiding. I, for one, doubt this: few would have been in a position to make such arrangements, and fearful news would only have caused enormous chaos. The Germans' possible response could have been to start killing Jews indiscriminately in large numbers. Spreading news about an impending danger may have been justified only if this was likely to save more lives than the additional number of people killed as a direct consequence[7]. After sixty years, until Andrew's death, we had been still debating this.

Returning to that dreadful summer, it was filled with unpleasant events. As a typical teenager, I was not always ready to comply with

---

7   For more on the topic, see the Appendix.

all the rules, so once I was almost arrested for traveling on the wrong car of a tram (Jews were allowed to board only the last car). Several times my friends and I were drafted for labor duty; luckily we were always dismissed the same day. To gain protection against some of this harassment, we sought employment cards from companies working for the military, whose employees were exempt from many of the restrictions even if they were Jews. This wasn't easy, but a few times we succeeded in securing such a card, real or phony.

In the end, in September, we were ordered to enlist as laborers to clean up buildings that had suffered heavy damage from bombing. We had to report to a supervisor, who took us to one of these houses; he told us to neatly pile up all the bricks from a collapsed wall, which were lying amid the rubble all over a courtyard. With the help of a wheelbarrow we did the job in two days, and were waiting for further instructions. When no instructions came, we decided to transport the pile to the opposite end of the courtyard where we built it up in an equally neat way. This we repeated several times, until after three weeks, we were paid for our services and dismissed.

In the meantime, the attitude of the government became just a shade more relaxed. The Sztójay cabinet was replaced by another whose policies regarding the Jews were slightly more tolerant. The Soviet Army had already occupied half of Hungary, and the Jewish families in Budapest became a little more hopeful about surviving the war. Why would the Germans, half beaten, worry about the Jews now? But these hopes were somewhat premature.

All Hell Breaks Loose

In October, at last, Horthy seized the initiative and started to make preparations for switching sides in the war and joining forces with the Allies against the Germans. He was encouraged by the fact that Romania did just that a few weeks earlier. However, he organized the coup in haste and the preparations lacked sufficient detail. Also, he did not give enough weight to the fact that while the Germans could afford the loss of Romania, they certainly couldn't give up Hungary through which most of the supply lines to the front were running.

We didn't know about these preparations. It came as a great surprise, then, when on October 15 (Sunday again!) Horthy's proclamation was read on the radio, announcing that Hungary was no longer in the German camp and would be seeking armistice from the Russians and the Allies. We didn't believe our ears—could it be that the war was over for us and we were still alive? First, a wave of euphoria swept over us as we walked in the streets without the yellow stars and exuberantly greeted friends. The only thing that bothered us was that the German soldiers hadn't disappeared; in fact, as time went on, there were more and more of them around.

By evening, we knew what had happened. Far from abandoning their positions and clearing out of the country, the Germans tightened their grip everywhere. In Budapest, they did home-to-home searches and seemed to be in full control. Later, it was announced on the radio that Horthy was arrested, his cabinet dismissed, and a new leadership installed. To our horror, the new governing party was the infamous Arrowcross Party, and its leader, Ferenc Szálasi, became the "leader of the nation."

The Arrowcross Party had existed, in various forms, for about ten years. To the extent they had a program, they were on the extreme right, even to the right of Hitler. I remember one of their ditties from the late 1930s: "Night is chased away by dawn, / The painter has let us down, / He's not trustworthy, / Long live Szálasi!" The painter was of course Hitler, a reference to his early trade. Otherwise, the Arrowcross was hardly a party; they consisted of a few disgruntled army officers but mostly of trigger-happy teenaged thugs, adding up to an ill-managed, bloodthirsty mob. When we learned about this turn of events, we knew that our days were numbered.

The first order issued by the new government regarding Jews was that they were not to leave their buildings and had to stay in their apartments, draw the curtains, and refrain from looking out on the street. Anyone caught disobeying these rules would be shot. I no longer remember how, not having a radio, this news reached us. But I well remember the days of anxiety that followed. There was not much talk. To pass time, we tried to play cards but we couldn't focus. The tension was so unbearable that at times we felt it would have been a relief if a few of those armed teenagers had just burst into the apartment and killed us on the spot.

On the fifth day, at last, new orders came. All Jewish males sixteen to eighteen and forty-eight to sixty years of age had to report to the harness-racing course, a very large stadium. These age groups included me, my father, and two of my cousins from the same building. We had to bring along personal necessities, a warm blanket, and food for three days; we all knew that invitations of this kind were issued for stays of indefinite length. So when we said good-bye to those we left behind, we did it with a very heavy heart. Nevertheless, once on the street again after five days of confinement, we couldn't help but enjoy the crisp October air.

* * *

At the race course, we found hundreds of the likes of us, already waiting anxiously to find out what would happen next. We were grouped into units of about sixty, each with an engineer as a leader (a strange acknowledgement of the social standing of engineers), and each including a medical doctor. This was even stranger, because the doctors didn't have any instruments or drug supplies and this type of care was not typical of the Arrowcross "brothers" (as they were to be addressed). Two or three guards were also assigned to each unit, mostly Arrowcross thugs. My cousins and I were in the same unit but my father was ordered to report elsewhere; he must have been needed somewhere as an engineer. By late afternoon, all of us were assigned, and the units were ready to go.

On that day, our unit got as far as the Ferihegy airport, where we were put up in the attic of a storehouse, still under construction. It was here that we first learned some of the realities of being in a forced-labor unit. For example, in the total darkness, several members of our group who had to relieve themselves during the night misjudged where a suitable location for the purpose could be found. As a consequence, some of our fellows were on the receiving end, which they did not appreciate. That such an event would later count as a very minor irritation, we did not yet know.

Next morning, we continued our march toward an unknown destination. It was a nice day, and our mood was not as bad as it could have been. At noon, our guards allowed a rest, and the older of the two decided to address us in a short speech. "Filthy Jews," he began, "there is one thing you should know. If any of you would ever attempt to escape, I will shoot him, no questions asked. If any of you dirty pigs ever succeeded in escaping, I will decimate the rest. Every tenth, understand? So think twice before you entertain such a thought!"

As we pulled ourselves up from our rest with our heavy backpacks and took to the road again, we tried to reassure each other in the face of this rather startling announcement. First, we argued, the dog that barks won't bite. Second, we were in central Europe and this was the middle of the twentieth century, so the medieval barbarities such as this *smasszer* (as we called the guards) planned to commit were no longer acceptable practices. While cynicism was mounting, we still clung to the turn-of-the-century optimistic view that the level of technical and cultural development reached today eliminated the need for brutality. We felt that the guard's ridiculous threats were just that—empty threats to scare us.

The same evening, we finally arrived at our destination. It turned out to be the village of Dunaharaszti, some 25 km south of Budapest. The local Arrowcross brothers were already waiting and they led us to our accommodations. It was under a huge roof held aloft by many pillars but no walls. We were so tired that we slept well even in this uninviting, windy place. Our warm blankets from home came in handy.

The next day, our first job was to dig a latrine long enough to accommodate the needs of all of us. It was more to prevent health problems than for our comfort. This job done, we were finally led to our real assignment, which was to dig deep trenches at the outskirt of the village, formidable enough to stop the vehicles and tanks of the advancing Russian army. We started the work immediately, but after several hours of digging we developed grave doubts about the effectiveness of the trenches we produced. Yet, somebody in our group who could look at things from different angles assured us that our trenches would do the job just fine. "The Russians will arrive," he said, "stop at the trenches for a better look, and laugh so hard they'll be unable to proceed."

A daily routine was taking shape, which started with a seemingly never-ending roll call, then digging all day, and finally lining up for some not too nourishing supper. On some days, this routine was interrupted when a German unit stationed nearby needed some help. On such days, we were all trucked to their camp and assisted them in carrying heavy logs to a construction site. This was much more exhausting than digging trenches but the Germans, mostly older soldiers, were much nicer than the brothers. They had no illusions: all they wanted was to get home soon to their families. They shared their food with us and treated us almost as if we were human.

Another interruption of our routine occurred when the Arrowcross thugs invaded our quarters, ransacked our belongings, and confiscated everything of any value they could lay their hands on. This was not very popular with us. But at least it was survivable, and we soon learned to classify things in these terms.

Otherwise, we did not have too many emotions in the camp. No nostalgic moments or daydreaming about a bright future. We didn't have much time for such luxuries, and also, we all instinctively desensitized our feelings for our own protection: to daydream and then awaken to the reality of the moment would have been unbearable. We were under constant emotional anesthesia, and our time horizon was not much more than a day.

The next disturbing event in the unit's life occurred when, one day, somebody escaped. It was inevitable, I suppose. Our leadership, headed by a young engineer just out of university, spent hours discussing what to do next: to cover it up or to report it to the Arrowcross. In the end, the latter view won: covering up would have been tricky because of the daily roll calls, and reporting would prove that we were honest and responsible people who would obey the rules as fully as possible. So a delegation went to see the brothers, and an hour later, returned with big smiles on their faces. The thugs received them in a friendly manner, thanked them for the information, and assured them that there would be no repercussions. We all retired in the evening feeling that there was still some fairness left in the system.

In the middle of the night, we awoke to loud noises. Our friendly thugs had arrived, waving flashlights, and ordering us to get up and stand in formation outside the building. Their leader then addressed us, in a most incoherent manner; only one sentence was clear, that they were going to teach us a lesson. After the speech, we heard military orders shouted, people (presumably some of our leaders) marching forward, then to the right, then—silence. A few seconds later rifle shots could be heard, bodies dropping, but not a word. The thugs came back to us, selected a few young people and ordered them to dig graves and bury the dead. All others were told to go back to their bunks. The murderers left, as swiftly as they had arrived.

We could hardly crawl back to our cots. So, that's how it goes, that is the value of human life! Clearly, brutality for which no account has to be given was still alive, even in Central Europe. The guard who had promised to decimate us was not just issuing idle threats, after all. That was the moment when all of our idealistic naiveté disappeared. What remained was utter cynicism, the only way of looking at the world.

* * *

Next morning, we resumed our normal routine, minus our leaders, four admirable men, whose only mistake was that they were not cynical enough. Beside our losses, one other difference was more and more noticeable: noises from the frontline, incessant gunfire, shells hitting targets. The explosions appeared to originate from locations closer and closer to us. Yet, there was little hope that the front would just simply pass us by, and we would find ourselves on the other side, free. Indeed, one day we were told early in the afternoon to stop working, pack our belongings, and prepare to evacuate the area. The noise became so loud that the front could not have been further away than just a few kilometers. In the evening, we started our march northward.

We were supposed to go at quite a clip, but we were too tired and sleepy to comply. Sleeping while sitting or standing was never a problem for me, but this time I managed to fall asleep while walking, not necessarily a good idea. The original formation in which we marched completely disintegrated, and I found myself trotting next to our doctor, Dr. Bihari. He was a bright and energetic man, about forty (as a doctor he had been exempt from previous drafts). With quiet intensity, he described how, should he survive, he would grab the first Hungarian or German Nazi crossing his way and smash his head in and tear him into small pieces. I was quite taken aback and said that in that case we would be no better than the Nazis. He countered that he would be killing a criminal, not innocent people like those the Nazis had murdered. I remained doubtful, however, about the wisdom of encouraging people to take justice into their own hands (ever since grade four, when I was punished for it, I hesitated to be accuser, judge, and executor in one person). I don't think we resolved the argument, but it certainly gave both of us food for thought for quite a while.

At dawn, we reached Budapest. We had a short rest in a bombed-out building on Soroksári Avenue, and to my greatest surprise, my mother was there, waiting for us. We were in touch previously through illegal correspondence, but I had no idea how she located this building. Much later I found out that in dysfunctional societies, when everything else fails, miracles occur and people become dependent on them. For me, this was the first one.

Mother hurriedly told me her story. She was working, and living, in a factory manufacturing army supplies and thus was somewhat protected from the daily checks and other harassments the thugs so loved to inflict. She also had information about my brother, who was in a protective camp for children (he was eleven) operated by the Red Cross, but she had no information about my father. It appeared that our family was completely torn apart. The good news was, though, that she managed to obtain a *Schutzpass,* a Swiss letter of protection for me, which turned out to be a very helpful document for many of us who had one, as long as it was not torn up by some Nazi, which happened all too often. Mother gave me an original copy, which I still have (see next page).

That evening, our unit was marched to Budafok, on the other side of the Danube, and we were lodged in the basement of a champagne factory. We didn't find any drinks, though; they would not have done much good on an empty stomach anyway. Incidentally, my stomach did not need any external inspiration, it suffered periods of cramps every three or four days, some quite bad. But I got used to it; these nuisances were negligible compared to the problems we had to face most days.

My Swiss letter of protection

Translation of the document

SWISS EMBASSY
REPRESENTATION OF FOREIGN INTERESTS
DEPARTMENT OF EMIGRATION
V., VADÁSZ STREET 29

1631 / XXXIX / 1944

The Swiss Embassy, Representation of Foreign Interests, certifies herewith that

E N D R É N Y I   J Á N O S

is listed in the Swiss group passport for emigration; therefore, the person named above is to be considered the owner of a valid passport.

Budapest, October 23, 1944.   Seal of the
                                               Swiss Embassy

The next day, I and a few others who were the proud owners of *Schutzpass*es reported to our commander, luckily a military man and not an Arrowcross guard. He examined our papers and to our pleasant surprise told us that we were free to leave. He suggested that we join a unit downtown especially created for those who held Swiss *Schutzpass*es. This seemed to be a better idea than to hang around on our own.

So we left, in search of the Swiss unit. I took a slight detour and visited our last apartment in the hope of finding some relatives there and, also, to have a hot bath that seemed to be overdue. The place was empty; the women had been taken away a few days after the men, which I didn't know. I did know, however, that at least my mother was safe; about the others, I better didn't speculate. There was one thing left: I took my bath. Refreshed, I resumed my search for the Swiss unit and found it where the commander said it would be, in Benczur Street.

I spent three nights there but for some reason didn't like the place. With a few friends we decided to leave and join yet another Swiss unit (it turned out that there were several) where we heard we would meet quite a number of old friends and relatives. Thus, quietly and without much fanfare, we left and walked to a school in Tutaj Street, where in the basement we indeed found the unit we had been looking for.

The next day was my seventeenth birthday. In better times, this could have been an attractive milestone, but now, in light of some of my experiences, it could also have been worse. Mother visited me, which was soon to become a regular event. I even visited her once in her factory. In the meantime, we had to make arrangements for my brother who, with a friend, walked away from the children's camp fearing that the camp would soon be deported (at eleven, not a small decision to make—he turned out to be a tough little guy). He was given temporary shelter by a very kind non-Jewish friend, Juci Fodor, in her home, which meant, of course, that he was illegally hiding there.

In our wanderings we quickly became quite independent and street smart. Needless to say, during my errands in the city I was not wearing a star; it would have been too dangerous to go around the streets voluntarily identifying myself as a Jew. It helped that I did not look Jewish, so with some luck, I could slip through raids without being ordered to show my papers. Nevertheless, I tried not to overdo it. Some of us, as I learned later, were constantly on the move. They felt that in the Arrowcross society the only law was what the thug who happened to confront you decided to do on the spur of the moment: if he elected to shoot you, *that* was the law—and this could, they figured, happen equally likely inside or outside the house. Still others tried to stay inside all the time, because they thought this was the best policy for survival.

In a lawless society, it is very difficult to evaluate the consequences of any action.

My duties at Tutaj Street were twofold. Most days, I and two companions had to push a cart to a central location where we could pick up food for the entire unit. Most evenings, I was busy helping to forge *Schutzpass*es. We had a supply of letterheads and drafted a text in which we declared the recipient not only a candidate for a Swiss visa but also an employee of the consulate. My job was to sign the documents; I had worked out a number of executive signatures for the purpose.

A most remarkable event occurred during one of our trips for food. As we stood in line with our cart, next to us, with another cart, stood my father. After a few happy moments, he told us his story and sadly mentioned that his unit was slated to be transported to Germany within a couple of days. In my eyes, this was something to avoid at all costs. So I suggested that he should immediately switch to our unit where this danger appeared to be less imminent (somehow, all units seemed to have fairly accurate premonitions about their fates). My father came up with the excuses people often used on such occasions, from the roll calls to the assignments they had in their units, but I insisted and virtually ordered him to show up the next day with all his belongings so that he can join us. Next day, of course, I was quite nervous and anxiously waited for him to see if he took our conversation seriously. He was not a man to change direction mid-course. But as he appeared at a distance, I could immediately notice that his belongings were piled on the top of his cart. We were all happy, and left for our unit together. There he was warmly received; I must admit it was quite a cozy place, and the supervision was minimal.

After a week or so, however, rumors of deportation started to reach our unit as well. When these rumors became stronger and more pressing, we (my father, I, and some others) simply decided to walk away and move to places that appeared safer. In our case, the choice was a "protected house" where some relatives were already staying.

Within a short period, quite a number of such houses, protected by either Switzerland or Sweden or the Vatican (also, as I later learned, by Portugal or Spain) came into being, mainly in the Ujlipótváros district. With our meager belongings, we walked to the one at Szent István Park 14, under Swiss protection, and announced to our relatives that we intended to join them. Dr. Jenö Krausz and his wife, Gizi, very graciously agreed to feed us for an indefinite period. Space was not a problem because that one-bedroom apartment already had about thirty people staying in it, so having two more around really didn't matter.

* * *

Apart from the crowded conditions, the protected house appeared to be a pleasant place. Some six-hundred people in the building, of all ages and backgrounds, made for an interesting mix. And we hoped that our Swiss protectors would keep the evil spirits out. But it didn't quite work out that way. Already in November, Arrowcross thugs raided the building at least three times to verify that everyone there had a valid Swiss *Schutzpass* (a precondition of staying there) and, on the side, to confiscate such valuables as we still had. Those who were found without a Swiss pass were taken away; I shudder to think what happened to them.

Things became so unsafe by early December that it seemed a better idea to be on the streets than to stay in the building. One day, we—three youngsters—followed this instinct and roamed the city all day with serious faces and determined steps but without anything to do. It was a bitterly cold day, so we ended up at a barber's where we ordered everything from haircuts to shaves of our nonexistent beards, just to mark time in a heated (and surprisingly safe) location. Otherwise, safe places became increasingly scarce, not only in protected houses but in many other arrangements Jews used for their protection. As a result, my mother was forced to leave the factory and go into hiding. We received only a short message from her.

Later the same week, my father sent me on an errand to retrieve money from our old apartment in Buda, across the Danube. It was hidden in a book at his office, the only room which was not sealed. The journey was not without its dangers. Half of the bridge that I had to take had been prematurely blown up by the Germans, by mistake. A hastily built pontoon bridge was installed to replace the demolished section, and this was densely guarded by German and Arrowcross patrols. I was very lucky to make it, both going and returning. In Buda, on my way to the apartment, I passed the corner of Margit Boulevard and Kapás Street where the district headquarters of the Arrowcross party was located. The guard at the entrance provided a most ridiculous sight: he was so fully loaded with weapons—rifles, machine guns, and grenades—that he had difficulty remaining standing upright. My smile would have disappeared in a second had I known that—perhaps at that very moment—one of my uncles was being tortured to death inside the building.

Safety in the protected house continued to deteriorate by the day. On December 8, the Arrowcross again invaded the building and ordered all males under sixty to prepare their backpacks with food and blankets and stand in formation in front of the building. We were made to march in the direction of Teleki Square, an infamous place near one of the railway stations, where, as it was widely known, several buildings served as clearing houses for Jews before they were crowded into wagons. These trains were leaving for unknown destinations, but we had strong suspicions that they were camps outside Hungary. Finally, we thought, they got us too; there was no escaping from being deported.

We were all very desperate, and I felt I had to take my fate into my own hands. My father agreed to my plan, and I was waiting for the right moment. The streets were deserted—it was in the middle of an air raid about which we no longer cared. At one point, I noticed that all the guards happened to be either in front of me or on the opposite side; I decided to run into the next side street and disappear in a doorway.

But it turned out that on this particular street there were no doorways, not even a shop entrance, so I couldn't disappear and was duly caught. The guards took me into a doorway on the street we were marching along (that street had plenty) and started to beat me up with their rifle butts; how long it took I do not remember. I recall though that with my hands I tried to protect my head all the while. Curiously, I didn't feel any pain, not then and not after—apparently one can stiffen one's nerve-endings at such moments. During the whole experience, my only concern was that they should not decide to use their rifles in another way.

The building on Teleki Square where they took us was a nightmare. People were dying at an alarming rate, either from illness or because they were shot for trying, or appearing to try, to escape. Bombs were continuously exploding in the vicinity, and I could see one hitting a building on the opposite side of the square, a frightening sight. In one room, I found a book on the floor, a collection of opera stories as it happened, and to pass time, started reading it. I soon concluded that while operatic scenes could be quite violent and full of senseless murder, they rarely exceeded in horror our situation in this building.

After three days, we were ordered onto the street again with our belongings—this was it, we thought. But, curiously, we were told to march *away* from the railway station, in the opposite direction. As it turned out, our new destination was the ghetto in the inner city erected just a week earlier, a hastily walled area of a few blocks around the central synagogue where all the Jews outside the "protected houses" were supposed to move and which the Nazis could blow up when it was time for the "final solution." A little later we also found out why the change in plans occurred: it was just a day earlier that the Russian army cut the last train lines leaving the city—no more trains in or out![8]

The ghetto was better than Teleki Square but not a dream place either. As I recall it, old Jews were wandering on the streets in despair,

---

8   After this, deportations still continued, albeit on a much smaller scale—mostly on foot!

trying to understand what was happening to them. Curiously, there were no restrictions on walking within the area of the ghetto, a "freedom" we did not have since October; there were minimal signs of Arrowcross supervision. As a result, we could discover some families we knew, and visits with them provided us with some moments of badly needed warmth. We also took steps to let the Swiss Consulate know that there were some people with a Swiss pass in the ghetto; to our pleasant surprise, in a few days' time they negotiated our release. We walked out the main gate of the ghetto and nonchalantly boarded a streetcar (a remote luxury only hours earlier) to have a ride back to Szent István Park. There we were received with a warm welcome.

* * *

A two-week lull in harassment by the Arrowcross followed. During this time, an improvised school for the teenagers in the building was organized, where we had classes in mathematics, physics, and philosophy. A number of university professors, some quite famous but now reduced to living in this building, were our teachers. It was here that I was first introduced to the mystery of elementary calculus. In addition, I found some work I could do for the Swiss Consulate in the small office they maintained in the lobby of the building. My mother's visits resumed, and after Christmas, she decided to give up her much safer hiding place and move in with us—she was quite a strong character, not afraid of personal danger. It meant, however, that another mouth had to be fed, and our food supplies were fast depleting. On New Year's Eve, we had a modest party to welcome in the New Year whose end we might, just might, live to see.

Not everything was positive, however. The siege of the city had begun in earnest, and we constantly heard the noises of the battle: gunfire, explosions, rockets hitting buildings. Electricity went on and off; later, there was no gas and no water. Wild rumors chased each other. Little Robi Vermes, about fourteen, was the harbinger of news;

he would burst into the apartments exclaiming, "The rumor is … they say …" and was gone before people could catch him.

Some of the worst rumors proved to be true. Most nights after Christmas we were awakened by the strange noise of machine guns, not lasting very long but coming from quite close. After a week, we heard the news that, night after night, the Arrowcross had ordered the entire population of several "protected houses" to march to the Danube where they machine-gunned them into the river. This was confirmed from several sides; thousands were shot this way into the Danube.

Our turn came on January 5. In the small hours of the morning, several thugs forced their way into the building and ordered everybody to get dressed and head down to the courtyard. Only a few minutes were given to do this, resulting in tremendous chaos and confusion. People were running in every direction. I have often tried to recall how it felt to be ten minutes away from certain death, but I can only remember that it was beyond one's range of feelings. As noted before, human emotions are such that they cut out past a certain stress level:[9] we moved around in a completely numb frame of mind, not fully realizing the danger we were in.

At the height of the pandemonium, it occurred to someone that there was a telephone in the Swiss office that a few days earlier had still worked. There was a mad dash to the office, to the telephone—it was still alive! They dialed the Consulate in the faint hope that somebody would pick up the phone at that hour. And somebody did. That somebody advised us to try to stall the thugs for fifteen minutes, and officials from the Consulate would appear at the scene as soon as possible. While I didn't hear the negotiations it must have been difficult to mark time with the thugs until, finally, the Swiss arrived as promised. They came by car on streets that appeared impassable

---

9   Yet a few, the strongest, could retain their concentration even in such situations. We later learned that, thinking fast, some succeeded in jumping before they were hit by bullets, and despite the freezing water of the river and possible injuries, many managed to save their lives. I doubt I would have had the presence of mind to do this.

for the snow, ice, rubble, and dead bodies of humans and animals; they showed up in time to talk to the punks and dissuade them from carrying out their plans. We were prepared to die within a few minutes when, suddenly, the danger was averted.

It was a miracle!

* * *

We could not perceive the miracle of having been saved, just as we couldn't feel the danger itself. Next day, life went on in our unheated apartments with glassless windows. The temperature was near the freezing point inside and much below that outside. We did the elementary chores of carrying water, shoveling snow, and taking turns at guarding the entrance of the house. What we were guarding against was not clear. Three days after the first visit, the thugs came again, and the whole scene was repeated, with the Swiss officials again arriving just in time—they saved us the second time, against all odds!

The mood was tense, to say the least. While we estimated that the end of the Arrowcross terror could not be much more than ten days away, it also appeared that our chances of survival was not better than it had been three months earlier. We felt powerless and at the mercy of our fate. Deep down, we could not imagine that we might be killed—such is human nature; yet, we didn't dare to believe that there was still a chance for survival. And this, despite the fact that we saw ever increasing numbers of young men in civilian attire marching north; they seemed to be Hungarian Nazis trying to sneak out of the city.

As days passed, the terrifying noise of machine guns at the middle of the night seemed to abate. Instead, the noise from the siege became more and more incessant. In the late afternoon of the fifteenth, two German soldiers lodged themselves by a window two floors below us and started shooting at targets that we could not discern in the dark. In turn, the targets began to shell our building; it swayed quite noticeably at each hit. The racket became so bad that we decided to move to the shelter, something we had managed to avoid until then. That place was overcrowded, however, and dirty, with an incredible stench. After two hours of this, we felt we would rather return to the fifth floor, no matter how dangerous, noisy, and cold the accommodation there was. Others decided to do the same. We went up—and even managed to fall asleep.

In the morning, we awoke to complete silence. We looked at each other and didn't understand. At that moment, little Vermes burst in, with his usual opening, "The rumor is ... they say ..." "What on earth again?" we grumbled, with sleepy eyes still only half open. "They say ... they say ... the Russians are here!"

It took us long seconds before we grasped what he said. The Russians finally reached our district—and we were still alive!

Part 2

THE SOCIALIST YEARS

Liberation

We all rushed to the window—or what was left of it—to verify the news for ourselves. However, we could see nothing extraordinary. The square in front of the building was empty, covered with snow and ice—nothing moved. Is this what newly conquered cities look like? Or were the rumors unfounded? But just as we started to feel disappointment, a figure appeared at the far end of the square. He walked leisurely in our direction, and as he got closer, we recognized that he was a soldier, albeit in a strange uniform. The color was gray and darker than that of the well-known German and Hungarian uniforms, and the hat was entirely different, a fur hat. No doubt, a Russian soldier. Then a second came, and a third, crossing the square in the same, unhurried manner. For them, it was just another city, and war didn't seem to be an urgent business.

So, it was true! We were liberated on January 16, 1945, and not a moment too soon; I don't think we would have lasted another week under the Nazis.[10] But to realize what happened overnight was, once again, beyond our powers of comprehension. A complete discontinuity occurred in our lives; there seemed to be no link between what had gone on in the past and what was going to happen in the future. It was

---

10 For us, it was truly liberation. Yet, for most of the gentile population who did not suffer much under the Nazi rule, it may have been a brutal occupation. For many of them, the day was the first day of a descent from privileged (or at least safe) conditions to a life of hardships. For us, it marked the beginning of a gradual return from inhuman to human conditions.

like the curves of the much-studied hyperbola—disappearing in the direction of minus infinity and returning right away from plus infinity, without connection between the branches.

We spent the rest of the day brooding over such thoughts. We agreed that it would be premature to leave the house and explore the neighborhood. We didn't know how far the Russian Army managed to get in occupying the city, and safety in the streets appeared to be questionable. Yet, the next day, our curiosity got the better of us. A few of us ventured on to the street and walked around in the close neighborhood—if trying to balance on ice and avoid bumps and garbage could be called walking. It seemed that people from other buildings also decided to look around; the streets were no longer deserted. We greeted friends and acquaintances with great joy, adding them to our list of those who survived. And thus a new game was started which went on for many months: we mentally kept a tally of those friends who were still alive; about those missing we were, at least initially, hopeful. Some, we learned, were dead.

We found many of the buildings badly damaged, but the neighborhood as a whole was in a better shape than expected. However, soon something unusual hit our eyes. Brand-new posters appeared on the walls, apparently issued by the Soviet authorities, asking for calm, orderly behavior, and the population's assistance in restoring normal life as much as possible. This was reasonable enough, although the tone used was more suitable for children than for adults. But the posters began and ended with slogans, such as "Long live the glorious Soviet Army!" or "Death to the Fascists and Nazis!"—a style of addressing people we had never seen before. The announcements of the Hungarian or German authorities were dry, to the point, definitely adult reading. We didn't know then how fast we would get used to the world of slogans and how they would permeate our everyday lives for many years to come.

On the following days, we explored areas further and further away from home, inquiring about relatives and friends at their last addresses known to us. Some we succeeded in finding, others were lost; temporarily, we hoped. On January 18, the last of the German and Arrowcross soldiers were driven out of the Pest side of the city; in Buda, across the river, fierce fighting continued for another four weeks. It was eerie to observe the almost nonstop bombing of Buda (which we could see very well) at a time when Pest was already making its first, tentative steps to emerge from the complete stupor caused by the weeks of siege. However, as the first signs of life returned, there was no euphoria, no dancing in the streets, no strangers embracing and kissing as in Paris and other places. The reason for this was not only the general misery aggravated by the lack of water, electricity, and gas; there were two factors which forcefully emerged now that we no longer had to put up with the Arrowcross: we were all freezing badly in the unrelenting cold and, with our food supplies exhausted, increasingly suffering from hunger.

About the cold we could do very little, except to hope that the weather would gradually turn warmer; in fact, it was in no hurry to do so. Near the end of January, however, lack of food became the major factor in our lives. While by that time many had found other accommodations, we still lived in the "protected house," and at one point our family had nothing left except a chocolate bar about fifteen centimeters long. So we had to go by the self-imposed rule that each of the four of us was entitled to a single lick of the bar every day. This regimen lasted for four or five days, and I must say it did very little to reduce our hunger. In February, things became a little better when we learned that not too far from our place a public kitchen had been opened where we could get a bowl of hot soup at noon every day. It was invariably bean soup, and in spite of this daily diet I still like it today.

People resorted to almost anything to relieve their hunger. It was common to see men taking their turn in carving up a dead horse or walking miles in the hope of finding food in the ruins of what, at one time, had been a market. Enterprising people started to open small shops in abandoned store windows (no glass, of course), but they very seldom sold anything edible.

Actually, in addition to the cold and hunger, we had a third problem. It was the unpredictable behavior of the Russian soldiers, especially when they were drunk, which happened often. There was widespread looting, which appears inevitable when victorious armies occupy foreign cities. But this somewhat mild assessment was based on what we saw; later I learned that in many cases looting was done far more brutally than what our original impressions were. Rape—this happened quite frequently and none too gently. I almost witnessed such an event in the protected house (no longer protected), in our own apartment, where still some twenty of us lived. A soldier came in, immediately identified his intended victim, and the only thing that saved her was that an audience of twenty excited people was apparently too much even for his drunken libido. Incidentally, in the rare cases where a Soviet patrol could be located and called in time, they would take away the intruder and none of us would have wanted to be in his place. But many scenes of looting and rape, during and after the city's siege, were quite horrendous.

A less violent obsession of the Soviet soldiers was to collect watches. It appeared that no one in the entire Soviet Union owned a watch. At one time or another, almost all of us were commanded to surrender our watches, and some of the soldiers proudly showed off their collection, a dozen or so strung neatly on their arms. While it could be, at times, quite comical, the grateful people of Budapest would never quite forget this experience. Thirty years later, in the mid-seventies, a joke went around about the then-president of the Soviet Union, Mr. Brezhnev and his minister of foreign affairs, Mr. Gromyko, flying home from a summit meeting with the U.S. president. At one point, Gromyko asks his boss, "Say, did you see Nixon's watch?" "No," exclaims Brezhnev, "let me see it!"

* * *

In mid-February, things started to pick up slowly. At the recommendation of my girlfriend's father whom I met accidentally (and so learned that she was alive and well), I landed a job, the first nine-to-five job in my life. My new employer was the Smallholders' Party, an old political party now revived, not too big but of some importance. It was later to become a major partner in coalition governments. My assignment was to make out the membership cards for the thousands who were expected to storm the gates of the headquarters. My salary was most attractive: a bowl of hot soup every noon—bean soup. I was dismissed after ten days when it became evident that during that period hardly anyone bothered to join the Party.

So, it was back to the usual chores: shoveling snow, carrying buckets of water, chopping wood, and digging temporary graves in the park for those who died from illness, cold, or hunger. In the meantime, Buda was finally freed. A few days later, to my great surprise and delight, I met my old friend Péter Sándor, who was among the first to return from a labor camp outside the country, Bor in Yugoslavia. On his arrival, he was to learn that both his parents had become victims of the Arrowcross. Such discoveries on returning home were, alas, not unusual.

During the last days of February, mother had to be hospitalized with an infection (some hospitals already had wings that functioned) and an ex-colleague of hers invited us, my father and me, to stay with them for a few days. It was incredible to see an apartment without any damage, all the figurines standing intact in their display cases and most of the windows complete with glass, the rest neatly boarded up. It was obvious that we, haggard, dirty, and lice-infested, did not fit well into this environment. While a few baths in hot water (they had that, too!) and meticulous cleaning helped us to get rid of the lice, we still looked like a couple of beggars and after two days of rest we decided to leave. I could see the signs of relief on the faces of our hosts. Nevertheless, we treasured their well-meaning gesture.

In March, we finally found an apartment for ourselves in Lovag Street, a drab but centrally located street. It was actually two rooms in an old lady's apartment; she lived in the third, and we shared the bathroom. Two rooms for four people—it was an incredible luxury! Mother came home, too, so we could set up the rudiments of a real household. Some of my friends were even luckier: they left the city by train, by truck, or even by accepting a ride from friendly Russians (possibly offering a watch or two) to stay with relatives in other cities or villages. In much of the country, life was uninterrupted by war events, damage was minimal, and food was plenty. Two months later, they came back rested, well fed, and overweight. Unfortunately, we did not have such a place to go.

In March, too, schools started to prepare for the resumption of classes. Many school buildings had no major damage, and schools housed in badly damaged buildings were forced to share accommodation with others. I had to look for a new gymnasium, as the *Toldy* was in Buda and no regular commuting was possible across the Danube. Besides, my loyalty to the *Toldy* was minimal, to put it mildly. So with an old classmate, Gábor Ludasi, who didn't feel many emotional ties to *Toldy* either, we decided to apply at a very prominent school, the *Minta,* a "model-gymnasium" where graduating teachers practiced under supervision. After some hesitation that we might not fit in (just a few weeks after the city's siege), we were finally accepted. The *Minta,* along with the Lutheran gymnasium, were the two institutions in Budapest where most of the scientists of Hungarian origin who became prominent in the United States before and during the war were educated. When President Roosevelt heard of this, he quipped, "Why bother with these guys, bring me the teachers!"

I was deeply moved when I first entered the classroom and seated myself in the benches. It seemed almost impossible to worry again about the various past tenses in Latin or about fine details of a mathematical derivation, when only two months back our main problem was survival or death. And yet, this was the normal thing to do. Everybody in the class and all the teachers knew that we could not continue where we'd left off almost a year earlier. There was little left of the old arrogance of the teachers (although this school never had been as bad as the *Toldy*) and there was a sense of comradeship among the boys, which I had never experienced before. I was deeply moved, simply because this was the first time in a year that I felt like a human being again.

* * *

At the very end of March, I visited Buda for the first time. The Germans had blown up all bridges in the city across the Danube, but the wreck of one could be used as a base for supporting a temporary wooden structure, which was suitable for carrying military transports. The structure was installed by the Russian Army, and soldiers were controlling the use of the bridge. Civilians were sometimes allowed to cross; at other times they were turned away. It took me two futile attempts before, on my third try, I succeeded. I was well prepared for the trip: one of my arms was in a sling and I was limping with the help of a cane to indicate that I was heavily disabled. This was absolutely necessary: there were Russian patrols all over the city, and they often selected young people on the streets to carry out some chores—a little work, they said, which may have lasted a couple of hours, a few days, or four years.

As I was approaching the bridge, I ran into the first patrol. With my free hand, I pointed to all my handicaps, whereupon the soldiers allowed me to go through but one of them, with a sense of humor, indicated that some hundred meters away there was another patrol waiting and I would not be so lucky the second time around. Indeed, I could well see the second group. I no longer remember how, but I managed to get past them too, crossed the bridge, and started my trip to Buda.

The districts I passed through provided an incredible sight: the majority of buildings in ruins, streets hardly recognizable. I knew the area well, but at times I almost got lost. In one of the houses an airplane was lodged, the tail hanging out over the street like a piece of abstract art. The streets were completely deserted; having nowhere to go, the inhabitants continued to live in the underground shelters, even a month after fighting was over.

On my way to our old apartment I walked by the building of *Toldy*, my former gymnasium. It was heavily damaged but did not look quite as bad as most houses in the neighborhood. The principal, who lived there, stood in the entranceway enjoying the spring sunshine. Upon my query about the resumption of classes, he just pointed to the building: classes in this? I asked about our homeroom teacher and benefactor, Dr. Kresznerics. He died in January, I was told, during the worst period of fighting. He would have been my last tie to *Toldy*; now, finally, I could close this chapter of my life.

Our apartment was in a remarkably good shape, considering that it was located on the top floor of a building on Margit Boulevard, a main thoroughfare where the front line got stuck for over a week. Russians and Germans had been fighting each other across the street, and the signs of this were evident everywhere. Not that our apartment was livable; the ceiling had big holes in several places, and the furniture was badly damaged. But the books had only minor scars; in time we reclaimed them, and even today I have a few where the war damage is clearly visible. I picked up a few mementos for my parents and left the house.

On the way back, I went to see a small basement storage room my father rented just before we were evicted from Margit Boulevard last June, where we stored some valuables, including our most beautiful art books. We assumed that while the apartment would likely be looted by the Nazis or during the upcoming war events, the storage room would remain safe. What actually happened was exactly the opposite. I could find two or three books with only small damage, the rest were either burnt or stolen. I continued my way home in a melancholy mood.

* * *

In the meantime, friends and acquaintances started to arrive back—from Germany and other countries—most of them undernourished and many of them sick. Through them, we had first-hand accounts of the concentration camps at Auschwitz, Mauthausen, Bergen-Belsen, Buchenwald, and other places, places we had never heard of before. For the first time, we grasped the full horror of what had happened to the Jews under the Nazis. Of course we expected more to return; some indeed came later, even many months later—the rest were fast becoming never-fully-fading painful points in memory. Relatives were first clinging to small signals, sightings, a sentence in some letter, hope against hope—and then grieving for months, years, decades.

Life in the city became more and more normal in many respects. From mid-April, we had classes every day at school (until then, it was three times a week), and we started in earnest to prepare for matriculation, scheduled for the end of June. At the end of April, service was restored to a couple of streetcar lines, which made the commuting needed to carry out my chores much easier. (I ran many errands for my father who had re-started his consulting business.) We attended concerts; the Opera reopened. Suddenly, we had plans, things to look forward to—attributes that make life meaningful.

On May 1, I witnessed the first May Day parade of my life. Albeit on a much smaller scale than the ones to follow in later years, it was impressive enough. The highlight (for me) was a bus, fully restored except for the windows that were boarded up, with a sign indicating that it carried the complete leadership of the Hungarian Communist Party. The catch was the slogan painted in huge letters on the side, "Death to the villains within!" which had a political message by itself but was, under the circumstances, quite hilarious.[11] Later on, the Party never made such a mistake again.

In the meantime, momentous events occurred in the fight against Germany: as a result, on May 8, the Nazis put down their arms, ending

---

11 The translation does not reproduce the flavor of the original: *Pusztuljanak a belső bitangok!*

the war in Europe. That was the day hundreds of millions were so fervently looking forward to. We savored the prospect of peace on the continent that suddenly came into sight. Nevertheless, for us the war was over in January, and our myopic minds soon returned to concentrate on events that were occurring closer to us, having immediate effect on us. And May was also a memorable month at home.

During the last week of May, everything suddenly seemed to fall into place. The weather was glorious, and breezes from the hills brought the aromas of spring to the long-suffering city; finally we could warm up after the long freeze of the winter. It was the week when electricity was restored, bringing, among its many blessings, music into the home (my mother had carefully kept a small radio hidden at a friend's place). It was the week when my girlfriend, Mió, and I discovered that we were still in love. It was the culmination of a long climb; in the span of four months, we traveled from the rock bottom back to almost normal human conditions. The heavy clouds parted and the sun broke through. I was happy, for the first time in a long time!

A Glimpse of Democracy

Democracy seemed such a simple concept! I wrote an article for the weekly edition of our new school journal in which I tried to explain what democracy was, as opposed to the authoritarian systems we had known so well. I no longer have a copy of it, but remember well that it was an embarrassingly simplistic presentation that would not pass today for a fifth-grade essay. But we knew so little at the time!

Two features were highlighted: that in a democracy, leaders were elected and reelected, so if their actions were not approved by the people, they would be out of the job at the next election; and that the will of the majority would take precedence over the will of the minority. I didn't see any danger in this, wasn't concerned with the minorities' rights. I painted a fairy tale picture, and at the time, no one seemed to be critical of it.

We did not know anything about the infrastructure needed to sustain democracy. In fact, we did not know the meaning of the word, infrastructure. We did not know about the device of checks and balances intended to control excesses in both the political and economic arenas, and we did not know about the need for a strong middle class, people with an attitude of voluntary cooperation. We did not know how much time and effort it would take to develop a democratic society (whereas autocracy can be installed overnight by decree), and we did not know how fragile democracy could be, especially if not fully developed.

We did not know much about the freedom of the individual, other than it would be much broader than under a dictatorship. This was generally interpreted by using the simple rule that in our new democracy everything would be permitted that had been forbidden before. Jews would be allowed to go around without stars and travel on the first car of a tram; one could make loud derogatory remarks of the prime minister; workers could strike against employers; students could question teachers. That in addition to rights individuals would also have responsibilities was not clear. That the rights might sometimes conflict and how such cases would be resolved were aspects too complicated even to consider. In 1945, we were thinking in simple terms.

Hungary's democratic period lasted for about two years, until the Soviet Union decided to tighten its grip on countries in its sphere of interest, including Hungary. Without that interference, Hungary would have had a good chance to develop into a well-functioning democracy, a better chance perhaps than fifty years later when the transition was an extended and painful affair indeed. In 1945, more of the infrastructure needed for building a democratic society was there, the prewar middle class still existed (albeit damaged—it was then systematically destroyed during the next forty years). Foundations of a parliamentary democracy were laid; several independent political parties established; and in November 1945, free elections were held in which the Communists received less than 17 percent of the vote. And while a succession of governments had their share of problems and even scandals, they also managed to bring an extraordinary inflation under control (with a Communist minister in charge, of which much was made later).

It was an incredible feeling to live in freedom and go about our business without having to endure limitations and being at every step exposed to dangers as during the Nazi occupation. This was quite a change after years of nervously watching and trying to interpret every political turn, every official announcement ("Is it good for us?" used to be an ever-recurring question in conversations). As a consequence, many of us started to keep events of daily politics at arm's length—now we could afford to do so. My father and I obtained much of our political information from the weekly column by Béla Zsolt in the paper *Világ,* a center-left journal. Zsolt was an eloquent commentator with an irresistible rhetoric—boy, did he know how to write! I often found his opinions hard to refute. Otherwise, we lived the lives of carefree teenagers making up for the years lost, and for the following two years or so, our daily schedule became very crowded indeed. We regularly attended concerts, theatrical events, and parties; we visited friends, or they visited us, almost every day (this was the only way to keep in touch—there were hardly any private telephones).

Despite our easygoing attitude, we—and many of my parents' generation—were also under the spell of the mounting drive to rebuild the city, rebuild the country. It was to be a nonpartisan effort; yet, the Communist Party exploited the situation, declaring themselves the leaders of the reconstruction. This and their professed anti-Nazi stance were designed to increase their popularity, and the ploy worked quite well.

Not all of my friends excluded politics from their lives. Some were drawn to the Communist Party for ideological reasons, others were in touch with, or were even members of, the secret police, driven by a burning desire to ferret out ex-Nazis and bring them to justice. There was much bitterness among the ex-victims of Nazis, especially if they had had to suffer the loss of close family members. Divisions in society slowly emerged, which later became dominant forces in our lives.

* * *

Another thing we had to learn was that in a democratic society we had choices, and it was often up to us to select the next course of events. We could even choose the option of saying "no"—a dangerous choice in a dictatorship. Speaking for myself, I must admit that I made several poor decisions before I learned to cope with this newfound freedom (and by that time it was too late; the freedom of choice was again taken away from us). The following incident serves as an illustration of how unprepared I was to resist pressure, especially from my peers, and to make the right decision.

At the *Minta,* my new school, the resident Roman Catholic priest had been allegedly as unpleasant and abusive to the Jews during the Nazi years as the Reverend Petró at *Toldy.* One day, my classmates approached me with a document listing some of these incidents and suggested that I, too, sign it; they intended to submit the accusations to the appropriate authorities (the police, I guess). I was surprised at the request and countered that since I had not been at the *Minta* during those years I could not possibly be a witness to this man's past behavior. So my friends left, but returned the next day saying that I should sign anyway; they needed as many signatures as possible, and I should believe them that everything in the document was true. They put such a pressure on me that finally I was too weak to refuse and signed. A moment later, I knew that I should not have done it. I tried to retrieve the paper and cross out my name but it was already gone. I became extremely distressed, walked the streets for a couple of hours, went to a movie to clear my mind, and lost sleep over the incident. The memory of it still lingers on.

In general, however, I enjoyed my days at *Minta.* My affiliation there concluded with successful matriculation exams. In the fall, we (including new and old friends like Andrew Elek and Gábor Ludasi) were accepted for enrolment at the Technical University. A new phase in our lives started.

I found university life very much to my liking. Classes were stimulating, and so was the company of many of my classmates. Yet in the fall of 1945, conditions were far from normal, and the necessity of coping with hurdles caused by the effects of war posed extra challenges. One such challenge was that the glass ceiling of the auditorium where the chemistry lectures were given was completely broken, rendering the hall useless on a rainy day. We had chemistry three times a week from eight to ten in the morning, if it was not raining. This was far too early for comfort and it was aggravated by the monotone of the professor, the most boring teacher I ever had. We felt a strong urge to skip these classes, an urge that was reinforced when we discovered that in the Hotel Gellért across the street one could rent bathrooms and have warm baths for a very small fee. A hot bath was still an extreme luxury; in most homes there was no hot water yet. So, a few of us took full advantage of this opportunity, available to us in any weather, and we soon became the cleanest people in town. In addition, we managed to pass the chemistry test—by just a hairbreadth.

In the fall of 1946, we decided to leave the old lady we had roomed with and moved to a newly restored four-room apartment, our most bourgeois accommodation after liberation. There was a bedroom for my parents, a living room, and a dining room; the fourth room I had to share with my brother. This arrangement was, for many reasons, uncomfortable but not unusual. The American practice that all children in a family should have separate rooms was not feasible in Budapest (even if the "children" were near twenty) and, thus, quite unknown at the time.

Democracy in Hungary lasted, more or less, until the summer of 1947. Perhaps the last time we were able to enjoy its benefits was in August of that year when we obtained passports with no difficulty for a vacation trip to Yugoslavia, to the Adriatic resort town of Opatija (called Abbazia before the war when it belonged to Italy). It was a group tour—freedom did not extend to allowing individual trips—but what a glorious experience it was! This was the first time in my life, at almost twenty, that I saw the sea. On the first day already we formed a small group, five or six, and hung out together—it was great fun, and my social skills improved quite a lot. Needless to say, we planned another trip for 1948, but by then times had changed and we were forced to give up on our dreams.

The Communist Takeover

In a candid moment after the fact, the leader of the Hungarian Communist Party, Mátyás Rákosi, described the tactics he used to take over the country and consolidate his power. It was done slice by slice, he said; the approach was often called "salami tactics." First, he made sure that Communists were installed into key positions in the coalition, then he forced the large-scale nationalization of industry and agriculture, and finally he went after rival parties, sliced them into fractions, and merged many of these into his own party.

One of the consequences of this gradual takeover was that the population, too, became increasingly split into two groups: those who sympathized with the Communists and those who didn't. This "us and them" mentality was not invented by Rákosi, it has been used by many others before and since (the most recent examples were Milosević in Yugoslavia, Orbán in Hungary and—dare I say it?—G.W. Bush). The usual connotation was that all those who were not with "us" were with "them" and had to be treated as enemies. Inevitably, such a polarization had an effect on the lives of us all. Life at the university, pleasant until 1947, became tense and dominated by loud and aggressive Party members who made up for their lack of professional achievements by exercising their newly gained political power. The leader of this noisy group was feared by all at the university. We all had to attend seminars and were regularly brainwashed by the media. It all boiled down to having to answer a simple question, "Are you with us?" It was increasingly difficult to stay apolitical. We had to stand up and be counted.

Many of my friends had already applied for Party membership. Generally, the Party was joined for three reasons: agreement with the Party's philosophy and program; self-protection—to secure advance warnings of some of the Party's actions, especially if they represented a threat or danger to some people; and sheer opportunism to gain promotions, trips or an apartment. Most of my friends did it for the first or second reason—very few of them were opportunists.

Actually, another reason existed for joining the Party, less tangible than the three reasons above. It was that the Party (similarly to a church) provided its members with a sense of belonging, a community spirit. For those of Jewish origin, this may have been an important factor. Because of their isolation during the Nazi times, Jews felt rootless and their desire to belong, so important for teenagers and even for many adults was mostly left unsatisfied. In some schools (but not in Buda where *Toldy* was) Boy Scout units with mainly Jewish members could satisfy this need to some extent. After the war, many of the young Jews became Zionists, a movement that rivaled (and was hated by) the Party. Others still had no outlet and joining the Party could fill the need.

For me, the answer to the question, "Are you with us?" represented a dilemma. I certainly wanted to be better informed, as I dreaded being in a position where I never knew what was coming next. Also, I had no serious objections to the Party's philosophy and program. The Communist teaching about society's past and future development seemed to be plausible if not absolutely convincing in all details; the credo included the history of the exploitation of many by a few and the inevitable resolution in the future—a socialist society turning into a communist one, with no borders, no states, and everybody working according to his abilities and being catered to according to his needs. Some of my economist friends warned that this was an impossible blueprint, but then I figured that economics was such a soft science;

almost any of its theories could both be proved or disproved. It so happened they had a good point but that was not obvious then.

We were given an expurgated version of the Party's history to read, so we did not know about Stalin's ruthless dealings with minorities, about the great purges, and about the gulag. Had we known these things, we would have at least privately discussed them, and our conclusions might have been different. But we were duped. We were also told that the party was the only force in the country that had been consistently fighting against the remains of Nazi ideology and against the ex-Nazis still lurking around. This aspect appealed to me. And in matters of religion, I was ahead of the Party.

I cannot deny that the opportunity to "belong" had quite a pull for me. This was the first (and last) time in my life that I seriously considered yielding to this temptation. Yet, I realized that belonging to a group with a strong ideology also had a flip side: it often robbed a person of the opportunity to make individual assessments and decisions. Those who belonged were, by definition, followers.

In the end, this was the only thing that kept me from joining. Even if I were in agreement with the Party's principles and agenda, what was the guarantee that I would continue to do so in the future? It was known that once in, one could not resign from the Party without facing dire consequences. No one ever did. Would I not be offering a blank check? Many with whom I consulted minimized the significance of this concern. The advice was, "Just roll along and all will be fine!" Finally, I lost patience with my indecision and, in April 1948, applied for membership. A few weeks later, my application was accepted.

* * *

There seemed to be no change in my life as a Party member. I didn't feel happier or more relaxed. I continued as a final-year engineering student, somewhat behind with preparing for the exams. My lifestyle hadn't changed much either (not yet) from what I described earlier: concerts almost every day, busy social life, attending university lectures and preparing for them, attending an increasing number of political meetings, and other obligations to look after. Reading these pages of my diaries, I am amazed where I got the energy to do all this; but then, at twenty, one has an abundance of energy one can burn seemingly without punishment.

Near the end of 1948, I received an important assignment from the Party. I was asked to organize a program for procuring and publishing lecture notes in subjects where no other literature was available; these notes would then be distributed at nominal cost. The task was quite a challenge, and I soon became a one-man publishing empire. I published about half a dozen excellent lecture notes, well-written and beautifully typed, and was quite proud of my products. As authors, I engaged the best talent I could find; in one case, it was the retired professor Emil Schimanek, an authority in thermodynamics, who was one of my father's teachers during the 1910s. He managed to write a very clear text on a subject which until then was a complete mystery to us: our lecturer used to provide his explanations in an incomprehensible mumble. Visits with Prof. Schimanek were a delight; he loved to discuss good old times that, for him, were decades well before I was born. He also liked to gossip.

In time, it became nearly impossible for one person to carry out all the duties associated with this publishing venture, especially if that person was still a student. My assignment ended after two years when a whole office was established to carry on with the job.

During the same period, the university underwent unprecedented growth. In a politically motivated action, many students from the "working class" who took fast courses in high-school subjects and were now ready to enter university had to be accommodated. As a consequence, the teaching staff had to be increased and, early in 1949, some of the best students in the senior classes were assigned to various institutes at the university as teaching assistants. While the Party's hand was very much in it, the new assistants were not all Party members; they were selected more for ability than for political loyalty to prevent professors from complaining. I was one of those selected and, on April 1, 1949, had to report to Prof. Szentmártony at the First Mathematical Institute. That is the date from which I count my (almost) continuous employment.

I was quite busy at the Institute. I had to regularly look after three study groups, which meant giving miniclasses where I had to repeat the professor's lectures in a simple language (his style was highly precise but excruciatingly intricate) and conduct lab sessions where numerical examples were solved. In addition to teaching and marking home assignments I also had a political job: once a week I had to preside over a session of the "Friends of *Szabad Nép*" (the Party's news organ) where members of the Institute had to discuss the most important events of the week. I had to start the meetings at seven thirty in the morning, and, perhaps because of this, they were boring sessions during which we took great pains to contribute meaningless but politically correct statements. I never saw half a dozen mathematicians suddenly so interested in the latest agricultural developments!

One of my new duties was to take part in conducting exams (traditionally oral exams) at the end of every semester. This may appear to some as a pleasant power game, but it was far from it: we behaved with extreme politeness and often tried to add more questions to explore the limits of the applicant's knowledge. When it came to the inevitable and I had to fail someone, it was a most unpleasant moment for both of us. The experience was made worse, in many cases, by the student's pleading for more questions, or just one, a single one that might save him. In such cases I was resolved to stand my ground. Women could be even worse: they broke into tears that soon became torrents, then seated themselves in a corner of the room and continued with the sobbing without the slightest pause. Coming back from lunch one afternoon, I found four women, victims of the morning session, engaged in heartbreaking weeping in the four corners of the room where the exams were to continue, making it quite impossible to ask a question, and more so to provide an intelligent answer. There was nothing I could do about it.

At another time, a young man was getting close to being failed—he didn't seem to have the faintest knowledge of what we were working on during the semester. As I walked up to the blackboard to correct something, he came near and whispered to me: "Perhaps you remember Dr. Bihari with whom, at the labor camp in '44, you walked all night to get back to Pest, and the two of you had an interesting conversation. I am his son." Well, this was below the belt. I became angry: it still holds, I pointed out to him in a low voice, that as a Jew he has to work twice as hard as the others to reach the same standing and acknowledgement. I lifted my pen, but some inner force made me enter "passed," instead of "failed" which was what he deserved. The only explanation I could give (then as now) was that it would have felt like committing fratricide to fail him. I was not proud of the event, and he shouldn't have felt any satisfaction either.

* * *

Nineteen forty nine also saw other important events: it was the year of three highly publicized political trials in Hungary. Not being schooled in the history of such trials in the Soviet Union, we tended to assess them at face value at first. After an industrial trial involving a U.S.-based company, which elicited little public interest because there was no way to find out the truth, the Roman Catholic Primate of Hungary, Cardinal Mindszenty, was put on trial with very obscure accusations. There was no doubt in most people's mind, including mine, that all documents presented at the trial were tampered with. Yet, I had difficulty feeling sympathy for the Cardinal; remembering the role of the Church during the Horthy era, I felt that there was some merit in cutting down the Church and its arrogance to size. In the third trial, one of the top Communist leaders, László Rajk, was accused of treason. That was novel (as I said, we didn't read the history of the trials ordered by Stalin), but I thought that, while the accusations were probably false, at least the accused was not an innocent bystander: he himself had blood on his hands. The trials may have served Rákosi's goals but they also alienated many, especially intellectuals. As for me, they provided the first cracks in my Party loyalty.

Near the end of the year, Rákosi subjected us to another scare, this time directed to the Party members only. A new decree by the Party informed us that we would undergo a screening process which would separate the "true" members from those who had some imperfections in their (or their families') past. While (amazingly, I must say) I was allowed to continue as a full member, many of my friends were downgraded to candidate membership. Some took this very badly. A new wedge was driven between us, often separating close friends or members of the same family. At the beginning we didn't know how to regard those who were downgraded: were they pariahs or perhaps outright criminals with whom any contact could be dangerous? This gap slowly closed when nothing happened, but it was a typical Rákosi device, to unbalance even the "elite troops" and thus keep them in line. At the time we could not think of any possible motive and were completely confused.

Nineteen fifty, as they liked to say, was better than 1951 but worse than 1949. It was the year when our daily lives became thoroughly permeated with all the extra chores the regime required everyone to do. In addition to our work, we had to participate in a string of ideological seminars and attend countless political meetings. The seminars varied from the boring to the ridiculous. At one point, a course was organized on Marxist philosophy and its Hegelian roots, which was compulsory for all professors and faculty members, to be presented by several comrades from the Eleventh District Fire Brigade. It was a sight to behold to see our professors diligently taking notes and raising their hands to ask for clarifications.

The meetings were of two kinds. In the first, we had to regularly assess the ideological progress made in our institute and identify any new political education programs that might be necessary to increase the socialist awareness of our "workers." These meetings were open to everyone. The other meetings included the regular membership meetings of the Party. A main item on the agenda was a ritual called "criticism and self-criticism." Members were criticized by others for committing something they should not have done, or omitting something they should have done, whereupon they had to stand up and admit their failings and promise to be more watchful in the future. The acceptance of an admission and promise was then voted upon. A frequent accusation was that someone had been lying to the Party. This was regarded a very severe violation of the code. Penalties could include downgrading or even expulsion from the Party.

The devices of confession and obligatory remorse were not invented by the Communist Party. They have been used by other autocratic systems for keeping their people in line—every Roman Catholic knows that. People known to be guilty of sins are easier to manipulate. The family is another nondemocratic unit where the "people," in this case the children, are expected never to lie to their parents, to admit their transgressions, and ask for forgiveness. But some of this appears even in a democratic environment. President Clinton was impeached and almost convicted, not because of his indiscretion with Ms. Lewinsky, but because he was charged with lying to Congress. Complete and child-like submission to the bodies representing supreme power has been an age-old requirement.

* * *

Nineteen fifty one was perhaps the year when the Communist era reached its lowest point; it was a true *annus horribilis*. The Party's requirements from members and nonmembers alike became more and more cruel and impossible. Operating under the principle that the end justifies the means, people were ordered to be ever so vigilant and report anything they found suspicious. This included denouncing friends and even parents if necessary. Needless to say, the atmosphere became poisoned. If I had cracks in my beliefs so far, these cracks now became wide gaps. But this was not all.

Coming out from a concert on a balmy May evening, I ran into Péter Sándor who pulled me aside:

"Did you hear the latest?"

"No," I said, "what happened?" He paused for a moment.

"Well, for the last week they have been knocking at peoples' doors at dawn, ordering them to pack their personal belongings and be ready by the afternoon when a truck would pick them up and take them to some unknown destination." My face turned white.

"What people?"

"It is hard to tell," he said. "Mostly ex-capitalists or others whom they consider enemies. But some didn't fit these categories."

I could hardly control my voice: "Where are they taken?"

"They are being deported. The rumor is, though, that they will stay inside the country."

Deportation—what a *déjà vu*! My mood turned black. And, come to think of it, this was not just other people's problem, it could happen to us, too, for all we knew!

But Péter had more to say. "Did you hear the latest joke?"

"No," I said.

"It goes like this: In Moscow, celebrations are underway to commemorate the victory of the Soviet Army in the last war. In the Red Square, crack units are standing in formation in front of a reviewing stand. Comrade Stalin is just about to begin his speech, when a tremendous sneeze is heard from somewhere among the soldiers. 'Who was it?' demands Stalin. Silence. He raises his voice: 'Who was it?'—no reply. He bellows the question a third time—nothing. 'Very well, I'll teach you a lesson!' and orders every tenth in the first row to be shot. Special unit comes forward, bang-bang-bang, the dead are taken away, the pavement is washed up, and Stalin is ready to start his speech. A monumental sneeze interrupts him again. 'Who did it?'—no answer. Question repeated, silence. Special unit in, bang-bang-bang, the dead out, blood washed up. Stalin is ready to start, a sneeze again. 'Who was it?' This time, a young soldier in the last row raises his arm: 'It was me, Comrade Stalin, it was me, all three times.' 'Bring him up here!' roars Stalin. The guy is grabbed, taken to the podium, half dead. 'My dear friend,' says Stalin, 'if you have such a bad cold, why did you not stay at home on a windy day like this? You could easily develop pneumonia! Don't you know that in our society the supreme assets are the humans?'"

The joke was a twist on the well-known slogan, "For us, the supreme assets are the humans," a slogan much hated for its hypocrisy. While the joke was a good one, very few laughed when they first heard it; I certainly didn't. It was so typical of the times—terrible news and a blood-chilling joke, in one breath. No relief from anywhere. I went home completely crushed.

Thus started another of those dark periods in our lives, full of fear and incomprehension. We didn't know (or didn't think of it) that this was every dictator's favorite device: the simplest way to rule has always been to paralyze people through fear. Over the weeks, we heard of several acquaintances who became victims of this craze, and we could not see any logic or reason in the whole action. Nobody could understand it. One day I approached my boss, Professor Gallai (the successor of Prof. Szentmártony), a good man and a good friend, also an unwaveringly loyal Party member, and put the question to him: "Can you explain all this?" He hesitated for a moment, and then simply said, "No." We were all deeply depressed.

I was not only depressed. If I had gaps in my belief in the Party before, now my entire loyalty was gone. I was completely disillusioned, along with many others. Some tried to suggest that the ideology was still perfect, but the execution was erratic or even cruel; this seemed to be a moot point, it did not explain anything. I still had friends who somehow managed to maintain their loyalty, but after the deportations most of us were completely alienated. The nightmare lasted about three months; as it turned out, we were not on the list.

To describe the poisoned mood of those times, let me relate a true story. While it made the rounds as a cynical joke, its essence was no less cruel and frightening. It happened to a brilliant student of the university whose family background was, however, considered not quite perfect. He was tolerated only because of his excellence. One day, he made the flippant remark that "In our society everything can be attained; all it takes is to write a few petitions." This was overheard by zealous Party members and immediately construed as a brazen attack on the Party. A big case was made out of it, and the student was expelled from the university. His future was in shambles. In despair, he went to the dean for advice. The dean did know about the case, but couldn't think of any useful advice to give. Finally he said, "You know what—why don't you submit a petition?"

* * *

In July 1951, quite belatedly, I had my last exams and became an engineer. In true socialist spirit, formalities were kept to a minimum, but my acceptance into the ranks of engineers, I believe, broke some sort of a record in informality. Here is an account of what happened.

The final exams consisted of oral examinations in three subjects. The professors tested about a dozen candidates in separate rooms; we went from one room to the other, waited our turn, and felt as if we were on the death row. Normally, at the end, the professors and the dean would have a short conference, and the dean would announce the results; he would call those who had passed, shake their hands, and mumble something like "I declare you an engineer, congratulations!" That was meant to be a solemn moment.

In my case, the exams were held in the afternoon. Two of the professors finished by nine o'clock in the evening, but the third seemed to go on forever. Shortly after ten, the two who were ready, and the dean, became annoyed with the seemingly endless waiting and went home. The third professor finally wound up business after eleven o'clock. As he appeared, we all stormed him for the results. He declined, saying that the other professors and the dean had to be present for the announcement, and disappeared into the night. We were frustrated but couldn't do much about it.

I was of course quite curious and the next day decided to explore my results. I went to the university, but it was absolutely empty—it was the middle of summer. Finally, at the rector's office, I found one person, the office caretaker, a big jovial fellow, sweeping the floor. "What can I do for you?" he asked. I told him about the situation. "No problem," he said with a broad gesture, "come in!" He led me to an inner room where normally no students were allowed to enter. Apparently familiar with all the documents there, he went to a bookshelf and took out a big volume, the roster of final exams.

"What is your name?" he asked. I told him.

"Well, here it is!" he exclaimed, "Let us see!" His head disappeared in the book. After a while, he emerged:

"You passed all three exams—you are an engineer!" Then he stood up, picked up his broom and extended his other hand: "Congratulations!"

And so I became an engineer.

The anecdote serves well to illustrate the general drabness of life under socialism. This drabness was hiding behind the informality the Party so promoted. We were all equal, equally gray. We were acting as if in a black-and-white film, there were no colors; even the women were dressed in shades of gray. In contrast the West, on the other side of the Iron Curtain, appeared to be all colors. This point was brought back to me twenty-five years later, when traveling from West Berlin to East Berlin: only two metro stops, and I moved from a color film to a world in black and white. It was a weird experience.

* * *

In September, we had to move into a much smaller apartment. This was, partly, because we were not entitled to such a large space as we had and, partly, because our building was located in the block where also the Party's headquarters was located and they wanted full control over all buildings in the block. Curiously, the small apartment was the first where my brother and I lived in separate rooms, I in the small hall from which the living room opened and my brother in the maid's room, minus a maid.

Otherwise, there was not much good locally to look forward to. Neither did news about international events bring much hope. The Korean War was at its peak. The danger was very real that the Cold War could develop into a third world war. Much of the anxiety centered on the person of Stalin. An old man now, he showed signs of increasing paranoia and impatience; he seemed to distrust diplomacy and was more and more in favor of confrontation. He had a red button on his desk to activate nuclear warheads, not a red telephone to reach the president of the United States in an emergency situation. And the mood in the United States also turned paranoid, with regular hearings where those suspected of Communist sympathies were interrogated, many found guilty, and blacklisted (blacklisted! In Hungary, they would have been hanged). While our life went on, we were prepared for the worst.

In this tense atmosphere, old friendships could cool very fast, even if the former friends were on the same side of the "us or them" divide. I recall a close friend, recently married, telling me one day that he was expecting to be permanently posted to the army. I had never been a military type and considered this to be bad news. But not he; he was positively glowing with pride. I asked his wife how she felt about it. "Well, if he goes, I enlist, too!" was the answer. Clearly, they were more than just loyal to the Party, they became almost religious fanatics, an attitude I had never been able to understand or suffer. After this, a few years' hiatus occurred in our friendship. It was upsetting to see how even brilliant minds could succumb to some deep-seated emotional need.

Early in 1952, I accepted a new job with a research institute dealing with electric power system problems. Professional and political reasons prompted me to quit the university. First, I realized that there was little chance for me to become a good mathematician in the sense mathematicians (for whom I had developed immense respect) use the term. For them, a good mathematician is a creative person who can add new insights to the body of mathematics. I didn't think I was in that class; I could have stayed on as a good teacher, repeating the same or slightly modified material year after year. Second, the thoroughly politicized life at the university had become too much for me. I was happy to discover that the small research organization I was about to join was an oasis in the windy desert of politics, comparatively little affected by the Party and its stream of directives.

The Thaw

In retrospect, it appears to me that March 5, 1953, was the most important single day of the twentieth century. That was the day Stalin died. His last illness may have been known to his inner circle, but news of his death was a complete surprise in Hungary and, I suppose, everywhere in the world.

The import of his death was extraordinary. It changed the dynamics of the power game between the leading powers. This was not obvious immediately, but changes could be noticed soon enough. Already on that very day I felt that it was a watershed in the history of the postwar era: I was convinced that things would now, somehow, get better. And in the long run, this instinctive assessment turned out to be true: this day became the first day of the long decline of Soviet power. The decline took thirty-six years, ending in the complete demise of the Soviet Union in 1989; interestingly, the rise of Soviet power also took thirty-six years (counting from the 1917 revolution). Even if there is no particular significance to this symmetry, it is a curious fact.

I saw people with tears in their eyes and others with a hardly concealed expression of satisfaction. Two days after Stalin's death, a big demonstration of sympathy was organized where hundreds of thousands of citizens had to pass by a reviewing platform and express their deep sorrow to the leaders of the country. Outwardly, it was to be similar to the May Day parades but, of course, much more subdued in style. However, I couldn't recall any May Day rally as happy and carefree as this demonstration turned out to be. The whole outing became an obscene parade of joy.

In Budapest, jokes about events were instantly circulating. This has always been the case in dark times; it was the citizens' way of shoring up their often meager emotional reserves. They were usually light jokes, not heavyweights like the Stalin joke told before. One, for example, related to Stalin's funeral in Moscow, attended by official delegates from all over the world. One of them, Klement Gottwald, the Communist leader of Czechoslovakia, caught a cold on the windy stand, developed pneumonia and died a few days later. Budapest, true to form, was ready with a joke within hours: "No wonder Gottwald caught pneumonia; the knife was too cold!"

We did not have to wait long to observe the first changes. Rákosi was sternly warned in Moscow to tone down the "personality cult" glorifying him as the benevolent father of all Hungarians. Soon he was out of his job and the leadership was taken over by Imre Nagy, a stalwart Communist but more humane than the other leaders. Apparently, he had no axes to grind. And thus begun the era that became commonly known as "the thaw."[12] It was still Communist rule, but with a "more human face." During the next three years it had its ups and downs; in fact, for a short while Rákosi managed to regain power. But even he could not break the spirit of the thaw.

One of the first decrees of the Nagy government was to allow the return of the deportees of 1951. For two years, they had been forced to do menial work, mostly at collective farms. Now they faced the task of reintegration into the urban life, a task aggravated by the fact that job opportunities were scarce. The thaw, as it slowly permeated our everyday life, had many, sometimes subtle, effects on us. People felt a bit freer to breathe as pressure was reduced, and they regained some of their perspective that had been completely distorted during the darkest years. Writers and journalists were more willing to experiment to see

---

12 The term was coined by the renowned Soviet (earlier anti-Soviet) writer Ilya Ehrenburg.

how far they could go in critically assessing the system or some of its institutions. Actually, they couldn't go very far, but it was exciting to find a newspaper article, or only a sentence, we felt could not have been published just a year earlier.

One personal effect of the thaw was that many of us quietly started to skip the May Day rallies. Instead, we (with my girlfriend, Edit, and quite a number of others) went on two- or three-day excursions in the mountains, every year in a different region. Before 1953, this would have been a capital sin. But now, nobody cared.

* * *

In 1954, I was assigned to write a textbook on methods of protection against electric shocks, a topic I had been involved with for two years. Under normal circumstances, such an assignment would have gone to someone far more experienced than I was, but experienced engineers were busy or not interested. Since it was felt that a book on this topic should be published anyway, they picked me as someone who had time and some background to do it. At twenty-six, I was somewhat overwhelmed but otherwise quite happy to take on the assignment. I proceeded swiftly, creating rules for homes, offices, industries, and farms about what to do in order to minimize the risk of electric shocks.

When I came to the chapter where I was about to advise miners of how to increase their own safety, it occurred to someone that it would be a good idea if I actually visited a mine, just to see the real conditions there. Needless to say, I had never been in one. So arrangements were made, and one day we (others were also interested in such an adventure) traveled about a hundred kilometers to a coal mine, changed into miners' gear, complete with helmet and lamp, and descended in a deep elevator to the level where the operations took place. We entered a well-lit hall, with little trains running in every direction. I was impressed. We proceeded along a shaft, electric cables to the left, train tracks to the right. After a while, the shaft became narrower and lower, the lights fewer, until there was complete darkness and we could continue only on all fours, and then only by crawling.

Not used to such exercises, I seriously considered grabbing the cables to help propel myself, but remembered my own rule that this should never be done lest the cable shields were live due to some undetected fault. Another few minutes, and I no longer cared. Finally we arrived at the head of the shaft and, with our last breath, greeted the miners who were diligently working there. We were led back on another route, broad and tall enough so that we could walk all the way to the central hall. Clearly, they were not above playing a trick on us city types.

During my musings on democracy, I had believed, until this episode, that laws would be respected as long as they could be considered reasonable. Yet in the coal mine, I violated *my own law*, which appeared to be reasonable enough. I was compelled to conclude that another condition had to exist for voluntarily obeying laws; namely, that one would have to be able to comply with them. With no money and hungry children at home, one may not *afford* to adhere to the law (however respected) and refrain from stealing at the supermarket. In many of today's young democracies, economic conditions don't allow the emergence of a strong class of people who can afford to abide by the law, and, therefore, laws may have to be enforced, at least partly, by police methods. These countries have difficulties building a fully democratic society.

* * *

Now that the stresses were somewhat lower, many of us thought that it was time to sort out our feelings and views about the socialist system we had been exposed to for over seven years. The question we were trying to answer was, how much was left of our initial enthusiasm and loyalty for the system? In searching for the reply, soon most of us had to realize that very little was left of both. In earlier sections I did give a step-by-step account of how my loyalty had been, almost systematically, eroded.

I was reminded of the saying (attributed to Churchill), "If a person is not a Socialist at twenty, he has no heart; if he is still a Socialist at thirty, he has no brain."

To answer even the overly simplistic question, which was the "better" system, the capitalist or the socialist, we had way too little information, and what we had was distorted. From the official propaganda it appeared that the capitalist system was on the verge of complete collapse while the socialist countries were doing better every day. But from whatever little information we had about the "other side" it transpired that life in the United States, the leader of the countries with economies rotten to the core, was still pretty happy, the exploited masses lived in attractive suburbs, and the growing gap between the haves and have-nots was not about to lead to a bloody revolution anytime soon.

Thus, more and more of us gave up on the idea of thinking in terms of good and poor systems and, realizing that grave imperfections were inevitable anywhere, made an attempt to identify the "lesser evil" of the two systems. The result of this effort was predictable, especially if dictatorship (the form of government in all socialist countries), thought control, and the presence of a brutal secret service were factored in. As far as our enthusiasm for socialism was concerned, it was fast disappearing.

When I write about "our enthusiasm" or "our loyalty" I mean to speak for my closer circle of friends. Beyond that, the spectrum of feelings was still quite wide, although a general trend of disillusionment could be clearly noticed. The results of this became quite evident a year later.

* * *

In 1955, one of the taboos of the Rákosi regime was removed when we were allowed to travel again to foreign countries. There were restrictions, of course. The countries had to be "socialist friends," safely on our side of the Iron Curtain. Only group travel was allowed, with lengthy procedures established for obtaining passports and visas. All this didn't matter much; at the first opportunity we applied for the necessary papers to take a one-week trip to Prague. After a few weeks of waiting, all the documents were together and we, Andrew Elek and I, were ready to board the train. This was eight years after our last trip abroad, a wait long enough to have filled us with desperate hunger for travel, a hunger that has lasted to this day.

It took the train about eighteen hours to make the five-hundred kilometer trip to Prague. Of this, eight hours were spent at the "friendly" border station at Komárom, during the night, while nothing at all happened. But Prague was worth all these irritations; all we had heard about it was true: it was a magnificent city with centuries of history and no war damage—even socialism looked different there. The shops had more goods than in Budapest, and the people did not look quite as gray as at home. In fact, we were counting on these riches; the rumor was that during certain weeks one could buy bananas, something we had not eaten since before the war and were keen to taste again. Our hotel receptionist informed us that this was the wrong week but, on our last day, told us excitedly that yes, bananas had arrived and were available in a single store, in a remote suburb.

Already from a distance we could tell the store, people were forming a long queue outside its entrance. We joined the line, determined to wait as long as it would take. As we discussed our fear that the bananas would be sold out before we got into the store, someone in broken Hungarian inquired if we were standing in line for bananas.

"Of course," we said.

"So why don't you walk right in?" he advised. "We are not here for bananas."

"For what, then?" we asked incredulously.

"We are standing in line for potatoes!"

With some effort we remained straight-faced and got our bananas in no time.

The following year, the famous American violinist Yehudi Menuhin came to Budapest to give a few concerts. This caused quite a sensation, as it was the first time in more than five years that an American artist had been invited to play for Hungarian audiences. The event was immediately recognized as another milestone in the process of the thaw. The concerts were broadcast live, and as if by agreement many put their radios in the windows so that the streets resounded everywhere with the themes of Beethoven's Violin Concerto. It was an unprecedented demonstration, whose message was clear.

During the summer and early fall of 1956, the political atmosphere became more and more heated. Many public meetings were held, some organized by writers, others by university students; all were well attended by people of all ages and occupations. Most speeches were critical of the government, some quite passionately so, and listed, albeit cautiously, some demands for changes. Oblique references were made to the "Austrian-type neutrality"; this was part of the peace treaty between the Allied powers and Austria, signed only a few months before. In the treaty, the country's four-way occupation was ended and independence was granted on condition that Austria maintains strict neutrality in any conflict between NATO and the Soviet Union. Everybody's dream in Hungary was to achieve a similar status, but of course, no one dared to say it aloud.

I attended a few of these meetings and came away each time amazed that such free talk was possible without repercussions (the latter was not quite true). I had the impression that developments were getting past the point of no return, and something irreversible was happening. And so it was; yet when the climax came, it was a complete surprise.

Uprising and Exodus

Ctober 23, 1956 appeared to be an ordinary Tuesday. It promised to be a pleasant autumn day, and we all started our workday, as always, discussing the news and then trying to focus on some work-related problem. There was nothing special in the air or in the news. Even at noon, when we took our lunch break, we did not see anything unusual in the streets. But around three o'clock in the afternoon, suddenly things started to change. The windows of our office overlooked a main street, and we could see that people were marching in large numbers in one direction, as if in a hurry to see something extraordinary. The crowd became larger and larger. After a while, I couldn't contain my curiosity and went down to the street to find out what was going on.

I was told that this was to be a political rally, either spontaneous or organized by university students, depending on whom I asked. The vague notion was that we would listen to a number of speeches demanding more freedom for the country. The immediate goal seemed to be to proceed to the statue of Bem (a general in the 1848–1849 uprising and war) where speakers would be awaiting us. As we crossed Margit Bridge, several people distributed leaflets with a list of demands. They were mostly university students, and the leaflets were issued by newly formed student associations. The demands ranged from the sublime to the ridiculous. They mostly started by insisting that the Party should be reorganized, the government should be reorganized, the Soviet

Army should withdraw from the country, and an Austrian-type neutral democracy should be established. They ended by demanding cheaper train tickets for students and better food at the university cafeterias. Actually these lists were touchingly honest, reflecting the main worries of the students and the belief that there was nothing wrong with the Communist Party except for its ideology, goals, and methods.

As expected, there were speakers at the Bem statue, including well-known public figures, eager to address the crowd. Their messages were brave, but their style was rooted in the worst Communist oratory tradition—they were deadly boring. The crowd soon decided to turn around and move to the square in front of the Parliament building. On our way, however, the attention of people became focused on something new. We noticed that most buildings on the street were decorated with the national flag, and, as if by conspiracy, all flags had a round hole in the middle. For the last few years, the red-white-green flag had been officially decorated by the Communist symbol, the hammer and sickle; now this emblem was simply cut out (see photo on the book cover). Soon, in the eyes of the crowd the flag with the round hole became the symbol of the day. By the time we reached the Parliament, one of the demands of the crowd became that the flag on the building of the Parliament, the "official" flag, should be similarly changed.

So there I found myself on this huge plaza, surrounded by a crowd of an estimated hundred thousand (some estimated two-hundred thousand or even more) people. With patient insistence, the crowd demanded two things: that Imre Nagy should appear and address them and that the emblem in the flag on the building be removed. After a while, Mr. Nagy was produced, and he said a few words that, for lack of amplification, we could not understand. It seemed however, that the main issue was the flag, and the crowd appeared quite prepared to wait as long as necessary until this demand was also satisfied. For many of us, the effort seemed hopeless; there had been no precedent that such a radical demand would even be listened to. The Communists were masters of stonewalling. An hour, maybe two, had passed and dusk started to settle. The crowd did not budge and chanted their demand, at different times from different corners of the square. It all seemed in vain.

Then, unexpectedly, two men appeared on the balcony where the flag was hoisted. They removed the flag and took it inside. A deadly silence befell the crowd. I could never have imagined that such an enormous mass of people could be so quiet. After a few minutes that felt like hours, the men came out again, bringing the flag. They put it in its holder and began slowly unfurling it. Soon it became clear that the flag had a big hole in the middle.

One would have expected the crowd to break into a deafening ovation. This was not what happened. Instead, slowly and quietly, from all corners of the square, people started to sing the national anthem. It was completely unorganized, absolutely spontaneous. The Hungarian anthem is really a prayer with a beautiful, slow melody. As it reached my ears with different delays from different points of the huge square, I became engulfed in a deeply moving outpouring of feelings—people overwhelmed by the sudden recognition that the impossible might become possible. The whole scene was almost unbearably poignant; many of us were too overcome to sing, with tears streaming down our faces. It was one of those experiences that come but once in a lifetime.

Then, it was over. I could hardly believe what had just happened. I always thought that crowd movements were invariably manipulated by political agents. But not this time and, for a brief moment, I could witness a magnificent scene, a heartfelt human cry expressing the deepest hopes of thousands of people. Dramas in theaters have such scenes, but now, life surpassed art!

The crowd started to move in the direction of another square for more speeches, and I decided to go home. Emotionally, I was exhausted; physically, I was hungry.

* * *

At home, I had hardly had a bite when Edit phoned from the university. The Telecommunications Institute where she worked had a number of short-wave radios that could monitor police broadcasts, including those by the dreaded ÁVH, the secret police. She and a few of her colleagues were listening into these conversations and, by and large, could follow what was going on in the city. She suggested that I join them.

I immediately left home and arrived at the Institute a few minutes later. There I found a small group with ears glued to the radios. Police reports followed one on another without interruption, and it transpired that the latest move of the crowd was to storm and take over the radio headquarters. The police were absolutely helpless and did not know what to do. They seemed to know that some in the crowd were armed but were undecided whether to shoot, or even to shoot back should the crowd turn ugly. They waited for instructions and the instructions never came.

A short while later, there indeed was some shooting: we could hear it over the radio. But it was unclear who pulled the trigger and what the response was. The police were desperate and didn't know how to handle the situation. From what we heard, things were getting worse with every passing minute. It appeared that the fighting was no longer localized and larger areas were becoming involved. Under the circumstances, we all felt it would be better for us to go home, as long as we could still hope for a relatively safe passage.

We went down to Gellért Square in the hope that a streetcar would soon arrive to pick us up. One came, but to our surprise it was a train from Line Six that would not normally take this route. As we questioned him, the conductor just pointed to a window on the second car—it had a small hole in it and the glass was splintered. "There is shooting going on over there," he told us, "we are not willing to drive through those streets again!" With the help of the streetcar, taking a strange detour, we all safely arrived home, but the situation looked serious.

Next morning, fighting was reported from several areas in the city; the uprising was in full force. The radio advised everybody to stay home. We sat in the apartment all day, in a gloomy mood. Gunfire could be heard from every direction. From the radio we learned that Mr. Nagy had been named prime minister. During the next days, he promised everything, from a multiparty system with free elections to negotiating the withdrawal of the Soviet Army and implementing neutral democracy. One couldn't help feeling, though, that the poor man was following rather than leading the events.

A day later, I decided to visit my office; our paychecks were waiting there to be picked up. However, the trip to the office was not as easy as I imagined. There was no public transportation, and when I had to cross a wide boulevard, I noticed to my horror that the street was completely deserted, with good reason: about five-hundred meters in both directions, Russian tanks were stationed, with their guns trained down the boulevard in my direction. Although I wasn't quite sure, I figured that they would not be interested in a solitary civilian, and ran across the street. Indeed, apparently, I wasn't considered a worthy target; yet, it was a foolish risk to take. Many others, in other places, were not so lucky under similar circumstances.

In the next few days, the fighting started to ease, and we could go around inspecting the damages. There were exciting sights, too, such as Stalin's statue knocked down and hauled to a mid-town intersection where hundreds were trying to cut small pieces off it and take them home as souvenirs. Or the headquarters of the Party's leading daily paper, where the contents of the offices were thrown out the windows and burned in the street. Edit, an avid photographer, was everywhere with her camera, and today we have an interesting album with photos commemorating these events.

During the first three days of November, our hopes were high. There were signs that the Soviet Army was leaving. We felt that it might just be true that the uprising had succeeded and Hungary would become a constitutional democracy outside the Soviet sphere of interest. We met repeatedly with our closest friends, the Juleszes, Andrew Elek, the Sándors, Péter Lengyel and Zsuzsi Kádár, and with guarded optimism started to plan our new life in a free country.

* * *

All hopes collapsed in the early hours of November 4 (again a Sunday!). The Soviet tanks were back, and there was renewed fighting all over the city. The prime minister issued a desperate call for help over the radio before seeking asylum in a foreign legation. Many members of his cabinet were arrested. An incredible cacophony of heavy shelling could be heard and was to last for five days. We did not know who were the defenders who delayed the progress of the Soviet Army for such a long time. Apart from a few army units, there must have been a good number of freedom fighters around, but they were lightly armed and could function mostly as snipers. Yet, they could also destroy tanks with the help of "Molotov cocktails," special light grenades homemade for the purpose. By the way, I was often asked in Canada whether I had been a freedom fighter myself. Resisting the glamour that an answer in the affirmative would have bestowed on me, I had to reply: no—I, like all my friends, had stayed at home and practiced what we knew best, trying to survive. Most nights we were sleeping fully dressed lest push came to shove and we had to move to the shelter. Luckily, this never happened.

When we first walked out to survey the streets, the city was a most depressing sight. Under the leaden November skies we could observe new damage everywhere; it seemed that after twelve years we had to rebuild the city again. A few days later, I met Andrew Elek who told me in confidence that he was about to leave the country. Now was the time to do this, he explained, the borders were not yet guarded and the risk of being caught was low. This shook me; somehow I never thought of this possibility. I felt that I was too much tied to the city—its moods, its buildings, its bridges, its hills—to be able to leave it for good. Yet, when the meetings with our close friends resumed, this was about the only topic we discussed. Andrew had already left. Attitudes were split; some (including Edit) were sure that following Andrew's example was the right thing to do, others (including me) were not so certain. To my surprise, my parents were very much for both my brother and me leaving—it was a truly heroic attitude on their part, completely ignoring their own pain.

There were pros and cons to consider. The main argument for leaving was the virtual certainty that the Soviet oppression and style would stay in Hungary for the long haul with no hope for significant changes. In fact, we thought, there may even be a possibility of the government reacting to the unrest with new waves of deportations. But even if this fear would prove to be far-fetched, the prospect of having to live in continued isolation made us feel more and more receptive to the lure of the freedom of information and choices that would await us in the West.

In addition, we were bothered by rumors of the hitherto latent anti-Semitic sentiments again coming to the surface. We heard about mostly unconfirmed cases with incredulity mixed with fear. In all, this seemed to be a good moment for leaving Budapest, especially since it was heavily damaged and badly crippled, and so at its least attractive. Later, when more of our friends had left, a kind of peer pressure also started to exert its effect.

Among the arguments for staying was the very real possibility that, if we left, we would never see our parents again (and many of our friends). Besides, we would be leaving behind our cultural ties with the city, its language and music—our budding roots. There was also the natural fear of the unknown; we did not know much about the availability of jobs in the various countries where we might end up. In addition, we felt some insecurity about how we would measure up professionally in a "true market."

In the end, all of us decided to go. Within days, the Juleszes left, Zsuzsi and Péter Lengyel left, the Sándors left (after staying in our apartment for the last night), and we also started to make preparations.

A group was assembled, a date selected. The last afternoon, I walked along some of my favorite streets and said good-bye to each and every building. Naturally, this ended in a complete breakdown; I felt I would be unable to leave and had to cancel the date for the next morning. The group left without us. By morning, I recovered a little, and plans were laid with a new group for the morning after.

This time I put myself under emotional anesthesia, said good-bye to my parents (trying not to think of the chance that we might never meet again), met up with the other members of the group, and walked to the railway station. I didn't look left or right but walked straight ahead like a horse with blinkers.

* * *

At the station, we bought tickets to Győr, a city halfway between Budapest and the Austrian border. We were warned that if we stayed on the train past that point we would run into checkpoints where for sure we would be taken off and sent back or even arrested. So, we spent the night in Győr, at a prearranged address. The next morning Ibi Temes, a member of our group, and I went to the main square to see what could be done next. We received all kinds of unsolicited advice; everybody in town was in the same business, and all pretense of discretion was futile. Finally, on our own, we found a bus parked there with the sign saying "Sopron"—the very town near the border we wanted to reach. We discreetly approached the driver to find out whether he could deliver us there. No problem, he said; he was to return that day, but there was one thing we should know. The bus belonged to the Workers' Council in Sopron; members of the Council were here to attend a meeting, and he would drive them back in the afternoon. If the company was acceptable to us, we would be most welcome. Our enthusiasm dropped several notches. However, after discussing it with the rest of our group, we agreed that we would take the chance and travel with the comrades.

We boarded the bus at the appointed time, and soon the Council members arrived, too. It took them not more than ten seconds to realize what was going on. They immediately engaged in a lively discussion on the merits of reporting us at the next checkpoint. The younger ones considered us lawbreakers (which, in fact, we were) and thought that criminals ought to be reported. The older members were of the opinion that, if we were unhappy in Hungary, we should leave the country and seek happiness elsewhere. The argument was still going on when the first checkpoint appeared in sight. The bus slowed, then stopped; our level of perspiration reached record heights. The door opened, and two soldiers appeared; they inquired if everyone had valid travel documents for entering the border zone. The driver quickly explained what a distinguished group was traveling on the bus, and the moment came to speak up for any of the Council members who wanted to. There was an unbearable second of silence—no one said a word. The door closed, and we continued; the relief on our part must have been palpable.

There were more checkpoints, but no more exciting moments. In Sopron, the officials left the bus, and some even wished us good luck. The driver was so enthusiastic about the success of the operation that he offered to drive us to the border right then and there. It was an offer we couldn't refuse. We left in high spirits, but as we proceeded, some cars coming from the opposite direction flashed their headlights, so we stopped. We were told that the Russian patrols just arrived at the border; thus, it was no longer "open." (How everybody knew the destination of a bus running along that highway was a mystery.) We turned around and agreed to meet again next day at noon. Luckily. We could sleep at the previous place.

We were all there at the appointed time and place. The driver, Mr. Benz, brought his son along because, he told us, his son knew the forest near the border even better than he did. But first, he suggested, we should leave town in style and take taxis that would deliver us halfway to the border. Primarily, this would avoid the oncoming headlights signaling dangers for bus. That seemed pleasant but weird; yet, before we could fully realize what was going on, we had to leave the cars and continue on foot.

Illusions about style quickly evaporated. We were led through forests, avoiding trails, and walked for hours, hoping that our guides knew what they were doing. At one point—presumably not far from the border—we heard gunshots, whereupon we were told to lie still on the ground, while the son went to investigate. He came back, long minutes later, to report that it was a Hungarian patrol and that they would let us pass in exchange for some money. We produced the money and continued with our odyssey. It turned quite dark when, after a sharp curve, we came upon a wide clearing. This was the border, we were told. From now on, we would be on our own.

We exchanged good wishes and money and started on our way to the other side. So, this was the famous, the impenetrable Iron Curtain! While walking across the clearing, however, we also had some uncomfortable thoughts about it. Only a few months before, it had been a minefield; the mines were lifted during the summer as a Hungarian gesture towards Austria. What if, by mistake, a few were left behind? Nevertheless, we all arrived in Austria safe, at around seven o'clock in the evening. The day was November 26, 1956. This moment marked the second discontinuity in our personal histories and was the beginning of the third distinct phase of our lives.

It was pitch dark when we started to climb a hill on the Austrian side. We were on our own and promptly lost orientation. The thought that we might involuntarily cross the border again and get back to Hungary was quite alarming. We decided, therefore, to find a suitable spot and sit out the night there. Luckily, the weather was quite mild, and for a further source of heat, we had a flask of rum that we shared. Not much of it was left by the morning.

As the sun rose, we discovered that just a few meters away was a road that led to a village in Austria. We were about to embark on it when Edit stopped us. "What about a photograph?" she asked with an innocent smile, and pulled out her camera. I almost fainted! Had she been discovered with a camera in the border zone, she could have been charged with espionage. But now, this was not the time for complaints.

She took two photos of a ragtag group, with all their belongings in briefcases and shoulder bags, standing near the border on the free side of the Iron Curtain.

Our group at morning after crossing the border

Epilogue

IMPRESSIONS OF CANADA

After I completed the two main parts (on the Nazi and Socialist years) of this book, several readers of early drafts suggested that I should add a few pages on our first impressions of Canada. But, I wondered, would it not be against my mandate? Admittedly, we were still ordinary people, and for us, these were extraordinary times, not without unusual difficulties. However, by no means could this period be considered "evil." Besides, we were not pushed into the experience against our will; we were originating it and fully responsible for it. Therefore, I first hesitated to add this chapter fearing that it might not make a logical sequel to the first two parts; yet, when it slowly emerged, it appeared that the match was not so bad. So, here it is. To emphasize the difference, I called the new chapter Epilogue rather than Part Three.

Cities

Perhaps it is not surprising: one of our first impressions of Canada was that, compared to the overheated conditions in Hungary, we felt protected as if we were in a sanatorium. The exciting political events in the world reached us, if at all, in a much muffled, barely noticeable way. External events didn't seem to be our business. At lunch breaks, people did not vehemently discuss politics, as in Hungary; they discussed cars and sports. It took me close to a year to convince myself that it was not so important to read the news every day first thing in the morning; the paper would wait, the news would wait, and it was perfectly satisfactory to scan them in the evening. Canada was such a blessed place, far from the centers where all the "happenings" occurred; we felt welcome and safe. Even today, at times it still feels like being in a sanatorium.

However, not everything was that comforting during our first months in Canada. We had to face, and deal with, an enormous culture shock in the transition period. The contrast was the worst between the cultures of large cities, such as Budapest and Toronto (our starting point and destination). What we missed most in our early years in Toronto was the vibrancy of the city's life. To my mind, "vibrancy" consisted of a busy social and cultural life, and the population's eager (mostly intensely critical) involvement with anything that occurred in the city. Budapest has been, even during the worst years of socialism, a vibrant city whose layout, institutions, and lifestyle were modeled on

Vienna and Paris. The cafés and restaurants, parks and promenades, have always been crowded with people discussing politics (carefully, not to be overheard), but also the latest plays performed at the theatres, scandals, and all events of daily life. Everything seemed to be of public interest, sometimes too much so, when it came to gossip involving the private lives of celebrities or even office colleagues. That, and the overcrowded living conditions did not leave much room for privacy—physical or emotional. The Hungarian language does not even have a word for privacy, a concept certainly unknown at the time.

A story will illuminate what I mean by everybody's involvement with the latest cultural events. During one of our visits in the 1980s (still in the Communist era) we took a taxi to get to a small street in the Buda hills. All the way during the ride, the driver kept us in his thrall by an improvised yet very sensitive eulogy for a well-known actor of the National Theater who had died a week earlier. It was a first-class act and could have been printed word by word. Less impressive was that near the end of the journey he got completely lost, and we had to help him to find the street. A self-made intellectual and a somewhat amateurish taxi driver—how typical of Budapest!

In contrast to most European cities, Toronto and many North American cities had hardly any signs of "vibrancy." When we arrived, Toronto looked like an oversized village with no people in the streets; only cars indicated the presence of life. There was a single bookstore worthy of the name; there were no cafés, no tree-lined boulevards with coordinated, attractive houses, and no friendly squares where people, young and old, could meet and discuss events of the day. In fact, there were no squares at all. Everything was closed on Sundays—in Ottawa, even the public transportation was shut down. Very few theaters existed; there was a single permanent company. Good music was available, but the core of subscribers to orchestral concerts consisted of little old ladies for whom "going to the symphony," no matter what was on the program, was an important social rite. The city's social strata were defined by the WASP (White, Anglo-Saxon, Protestant) majority, and crossing the lines took an amount of determination very few had. People knew their places. They lived very private lives; public events, other than sports, were seldom discussed. Nothing seemed to be worthy of general attention. Privacy and comfort were the most valued assets, even in the less affluent layers of society. It seemed at the time that one could have either vibrancy or privacy, but not both.

We all knew our places, and if we didn't, we were reminded of it. In the spring of 1957, when the cold weather finally relented, we were exploring various neighborhoods in Toronto. During a Sunday walk, we found ourselves in Rosedale, a wealthy area although we didn't know this. There were a few apartment buildings around and since we were thinking of renting an apartment after having lived for some months in a rooming house, we walked into one which had a sign posted, "Apartments to let." A doorman blocked our way: "What do you want?" he asked in a not too friendly manner. We innocently told him that we were looking for an apartment. After an icy moment of silence while he was sizing us up, he declared, "You can't afford it." Without another word, we were dismissed. He was probably a good observer, but the treatment was humiliating.

* * *

In my letters from early 1957, just a few weeks after we had arrived in Toronto, a few topics kept continually returning. Repeatedly and with little success, I tried to define our place in society: it was hard to accept our almost totally isolated existence, especially if compared with the high degree of social, cultural, and professional connectedness we enjoyed in Budapest. Also, with some arrogance, I was wondering how we would be getting used to the "barbarian cities" in North America whose aesthetics and culture appeared to be inferior to what one could experience in Europe. Since we didn't move around much in the cold winter, we didn't realize how attractive many of the suburbs were, especially those with plenty of mature trees. This was a reversal of the typical layout of European cities where most suburbs were industrial and, consequently, quite ugly; for beauty, one had to visit the inner districts. The concept of "downtown," a relatively small area of high-rise buildings that housed offices and department stores but no residences, was unknown in Europe. When, after landing in Ottawa, we were bussed downtown for medical examination, the neighborhoods we were riding through looked like districts of pleasant summer resorts closed for the winter. We were wondering where the city was, and didn't notice that we were right in the middle of it.

Of course, things have changed in the last fifty years, both in Budapest and in Toronto. In Budapest, one can now at least buy privacy (given enough money); there are no state-imposed restrictions on the size of a home one may own. Shops display the widest range of selections. One can speak freely in public places, without the fear of being overheard by the secret police. And the illuminated buildings and bridges at night provide a more beautiful sight than ever. In Toronto, huge crowds had recently lined up for several days to inspect the newly completed opera house, a show of interest that was unimaginable fifty years ago (but so was an opera house itself). Several new concert halls have opened, actually more than needed. There are many cafés (with outdoor sections during the summer) and a large number of good bookstores.

A remarkable development in Toronto has been, since about 1960, the construction of a number of covered shopping malls where people go not only for shopping but also for socializing, food, and drinks. The modern mall is a North American invention, loosely based on the nineteenth century *gallerias* and *arcades* in Europe, the most famous of which are those in Milan and Brussels. From the outside, the American malls look like ugly fortresses in the middle of huge parking lots, but the insides tell a different story. Visitors, especially the young, find them inviting, with their great variety of shops, broad and clean corridors, many benches, and year-round protection from weather. They have changed the lifestyle of many people, particularly in the suburbs. In fact, the malls seem to be taking on the role of the nonexisting public squares in Toronto; they offer places where people can meet in attractive surroundings. Of late, European cities, too, have begun building malls, notwithstanding their many parks and squares. Clearly, vibrancy is no longer to be experienced only in Europe; Toronto, for one, has become a very livable city.

However, livable does not necessarily mean lovable. A lovable city has its own atmosphere, its characteristic way of life appreciated by many of the inhabitants. Often, sentimental songs glorify the city, its beauty, its landmarks, and aspects of its life—signs of the locals' love for the city. In contrast, the main downtown streets in Toronto are still utilitarian and ugly, expressing perhaps the original owners' doubts (in the late nineteenth century) about staying in Canada for long—nothing to sing about. Many downtown stores are now refurbished, and in some areas one finds crowds on the sidewalks: a good thing, except that they consist exclusively of young people. Is this because many of these streets and stores still lack in style and elegance what would attract the not-so-young? Architectural coordination of new buildings, at least on the main streets, is still a remote dream (of some; most people don't care). But see the new Bay Street, from Yorkville to Dundas!

People

I must admit that our reception in Canada was very friendly and helpful by all concerned—the authorities, individuals, and employers. This was far better than what immigrants who arrived five years earlier (or five years later) experienced. At the time we arrived, the red carpet was rolled out in many places for the poor "freedom fighters." In trying to find the reason for this difference in attitudes, I cannot dismiss the possibility that, in 1956, Western governments felt somewhat uncomfortable for not providing military help to Hungary when it was urgently and repeatedly requested during the uprising. True, by sheer coincidence, the Suez crisis occurred the same week and diverted the attention of the Western leaders. Yet even without Suez, I suspect that Hungary would not have been considered worth a potential world conflict—the strength of the Soviet Union was significantly overestimated. To cover up for the resulting embarrassment and restore their credibility, Western governments enthusiastically greeted the 200,000 or so refugees who left Hungary in despair after the return of the Soviet Army; many accepted large numbers of them with all formalities lifted. We didn't know how lucky we were.

The helpfulness of employers was, in the first place, due to the fact that they could afford it: the economy was at the tail end of a boom that peaked earlier in the fifties, and jobs were plentiful. Yet, in several cases, we experienced true goodwill, even eagerness to help. Universities jumped at the chance of getting highly educated young talent into

110

their graduate schools. Other employers smelled an opportunity to get more value for the money by paying immigrants less than the standard rates—engineers, for example, were often undervalued because they were not familiar with the inch-pound measurement system. But we were ready to go through some bumps along the road: on the airplane delivering us to Canada, we (three engineers, Gábor Lengyel, Péter Sándor, and I) had a memorable discussion in which we agreed that we would accept any job at first, even if we had to begin as shoeshine boys at a street corner. We felt we were young enough to restart our lives at that level if necessary, and then show gradually what we were capable of doing. Luckily, we never had to do the shoeshine bit.

In fact, in my earliest letters written at the time I could recognize that our financial position was *already* far better than it had been in Hungary. After a week in Toronto, we (Edit, also an engineer, and I—now married) both had jobs, each earning (the minimal) engineering salary. True, Edit had some difficulties with her first job applications: some companies were not interested in employing married women because of the chances that they would quit as soon as they would start a family; others were ready to employ her for half the salary a male engineer would get. Such biases were widespread throughout the fifties, and companies were quite open about these practices. Still, we were amazed to find that the living standard of ordinary people was at a level we could not imagine before. We couldn't stop marveling at the (then fairly new) supermarkets, with their riches and the incredible choices they were offering. In many walks of life we could make choices, freely, something quite new to us. All these contradicting observations often made me confused and tense: much of the time I was impressed, and some of the time, depressed.

Some of this depression could be linked to the weather. Even today, I would not advise anyone to settle in Toronto in January. And in those days, winters were (or seemed to be) much harsher; the gray skies could warm us up very little and the not infrequent snowstorms made moving around rather difficult. We got to work and back, though, day after day, but to think that this would be our world for many years to come didn't cheer us much. A summer later, our view of Toronto became more tolerant.

Another aspect that influenced my mood those early days was that I didn't find my work, and my colleagues at work, particularly stimulating. For over two years, I performed maintenance tasks in a never-ending series of electric substations; our crew moved from station to station without having an office of our own, not even a desk. Nominally it was an engineer's job, but in fact, most of my coworkers were technicians. They were all very friendly to me, but not interested in discussing anything other than cars, tools at work, and tools for home repairs. I was at least able to discuss cars, but otherwise our worlds were far apart. My bosses were suspicious of my ambition to attend graduate courses at the university (no engineer in his right mind, having a good job, would do such a thing, I was told) and were happy to get rid of me when, in 1959, I could obtain a more suitable job at a research institute—where I then stayed for thirty-three years, and had an office, as a scientist emeritus, for another fifteen.

* * *

How did others arriving in Toronto during the same period deal with the culture gap facing them? Educated people tried, and mostly succeeded, to adjust without much help, and in a matter of few years blended in with the mainstream of population to a remarkable degree. Many had elementary knowledge of English on arrival that, of course, helped. Others, arriving with (or later sponsoring) extended families that often included several generations could not hope to adjust the same way. Instead, they formed communities within cities, sometimes tens of thousands strong, in which they continued their familiar lifestyles; thus, in Toronto, a whole series of Little Italys and Chinatowns came into being. This solution appeared inevitable, but not so the government's multicultural policy (from the seventies on) of heavily subsidizing these communities and their activities, thereby unnecessarily extending their lives.

Cultural differences could be puzzling, rather than charming, even in small matters. Early in our time in Toronto, a colleague of Ukrainian rural background confided to the rest of our crew that he had a girlfriend with whom he was living and very much in love. He was the first man in her life. This led to the following conversation:

"Well," we asked, "Why don't you marry her?"

"That is impossible!" he said, "I would marry only a virgin."

"But," we tried to argue, "She had been a virgin until she met you!"

"No, she is a slut; she is having sex before marriage. I'll only marry a girl strong enough to resist temptation until the wedding."

Marriage to him seemed to be a matter of honor rather than that of love. All of us were taken aback—but then, we all came from different cultures. Yet, in Canada, are most of these differences worth preserving? But this is another story.

During our early years in Canada, the need to get oriented in this strange society was understandable. At the time, the choice of many newly arrived Hungarians was to participate in the lectures, balls, concerts, and other events organized by local Hungarian institutions. Fifty years later, some are still doing it. After a few early trials, we ourselves shied away from this, mainly because many of the organizers openly identified themselves with the values of the right-wing regimes in Hungary before the war. This shouldn't have come as a surprise: at the time, Toronto had a large concentration of former gendarmes and other Hungarian Nazis who preferred to stay outside Hungary after the war (with good reasons). They were catered to by many of the Hungarian institutions, including an incredible bookstore (by the name *Bálint*) where one of the bestsellers was a loving description of Ferenc Szálasi's life and death (he was the leader of the Arrowcross party whose "reign" I recounted in some detail in Part One—Szálasi himself was hanged, as a war criminal, in 1946).

And our need to belong? First, this need lost some of its importance as we were getting older. Second, in this multinational country, our discomfort from not having roots is shared by the majority, especially in large cities. Even in families who have lived here for many generations, the feeling of belonging is not very high; this is perhaps because of the isolated way of living that provides very little awareness of the community. We have not felt more rootless than most people around us (and since most of us could continue in our professions, we have not felt particularly "displaced" either). Third, some of us found a new solution later when we could travel: instead of having roots in Hungary or Canada, we started to feel that we might belong to that hard-to-define entity, the Western World of Europe and North America. I, for one, love and feel comfortable in a number of cities: Toronto and Budapest, of course, but also Paris, New York, or Zürich. At the time, we found this notion of "world citizenship" quite attractive.

Travels

Urged on by our decades-long hunger for travel, we started to visit new places as soon as we could. Initially, we traveled through Canada coast to coast, and then, in 1960, we made it to western Europe for the first time. It was a dizzying experience, to see Paris, London, and Venice and find that they really existed. However, all these trips did not diminish my nostalgic feelings for Budapest, which were only amplified by the very real possibility that we would never be allowed to see it again.

Not that there were no incidents which, at least temporarily, reduced my feelings of nostalgia. In about 1962, I visited the Canadian National Exhibition, held yearly in Toronto, and to my surprise discovered that there was a Hungarian pavilion exhibiting Hungarian products. I walked up to the window and asked for a few brochures. The charming receptionist explained that she was not authorized to give out sales material, only her boss could do it—but he was out, he would be back in ten minutes. Ah, a whiff of Hungary! While waiting I was wondering what was the use of having such a receptionist at all—after just a few years, I seemed to have forgotten the many layers of Hungarian office workers who were not given any authority. Ten minutes later, the boss indeed arrived, and had no difficulty in handing me all the brochures I was asking for. However, my request for an Ikarus autobus catalogue intrigued him—he leaned over and asked me in a confidential tone: "Why would you want to buy Ikarus buses, they are not good for Canada!"

To our surprise, in 1965, the Hungarian government announced amnesty for those who left the country illegally nine years earlier (until then, we had been convicted criminals). Thus, visits to Hungary became possible and apparently safe. In the following years, many of us took advantage of this and visited family and old friends, first with some hesitation lest we walked into a trap and would not be allowed to return, but quite confidently later. To our delight, we received the warmest welcome from most of our friends. As the stresses became reduced during Kádár's more tolerant leadership, once again friendship took precedence over party doctrine. These visits also greatly helped many of us to overcome our feelings of nostalgia for past times and places; they again became parts of our present world.

* * *

Our first visit was taking place in 1967, and was an emotional roller coaster. After eleven years, relatives and friends seemed to be all there, unchanged, without having aged. The city was there, too, almost exactly as we left it: buildings wore the same war damages; there were no demolitions, no new constructions (with the exception of a new bridge across the Danube and two new hotels), as if all would be just waking up from an eleven-year long slumber. Time Machine[13] kept playing tricks on me, as shown by the following incidents.

Early during our stay, I went to visit my favorite bookstore. As I entered, I recognized the spacious room, columns of bookshelves, classified as before—fiction here, nonfiction there, engineering books, medical books—nothing changed. And in the back of the store, behind a small desk, sat the manager, the same as eleven years earlier, Mrs. Uray. She noticed me, too, came out from behind her desk, walked up to me, and without any introduction or even greeting, very simply said,

---

13 H.G. Wells's miraculous device, described in the novel of the same title, which could transport people backwards and forwards in time with strange results.

"Do you realize that you stopped at the same column of books where you always used to stop?" This seemingly plain question moved me beyond words—that I was still recognized and, in a way, connected, after eleven years, shook me so much that, for a moment, I couldn't distinguish between *now* and *then*. It took long minutes to regain my balance.

In another incident where Time Machine succeeded in completely confusing me, a friend took me to one of the new hotels, built mainly to accommodate the growing number of foreign tourists, so that I should see the newest and latest. As we walked up the imposing stairs to the main entrance, I, completely forgetting about time and place, suddenly turned to my friend, "When we enter, why don't we play two rich Americans crossing the lobby and picking up a copy of the *Herald Tribune* (only sold to "western" tourists)?" This was a trick we liked to play in the old days. But instead of the expected laughter, he just stood there with an expression of incredulity on his face and was hardly able to speak: "But ... but you *are* a rich American! And you can buy the *Herald Tribune* whenever you want!" Then, reality struck me: of course I was now a "rich American," of course I could buy the paper any time. It was just that in Budapest I still tended to feel like a local—I was not in full control of my emotions. Finally, the two of us burst into laughter, but I was also shaken: I felt a bit sheepish but, in a strange way, somewhat relieved, too. These are moments one never forgets. By the way, after this incident, Time Machine has left me alone.

APPENDICES

Two Dictatorships

There are, and have been in history, many kinds of dictatorships, also called autocratic or totalitarian regimes. The common link is the total control exercised by a single person who cannot be overruled. This is ensured through terror, secret police, and suitable technical devices. The worst kinds of dictatorships are those which are driven by an ideology, a system of beliefs and values. In such regimes, significant pressure is exerted on the citizens to accept these values and conduct their lives accordingly. Frequently, the most loyal citizens make up the ruling party (very often, there is no other party). Those who don't share (or don't appear to share) these beliefs are often treated as enemies: they are regularly watched by the secret police and are, for the slightest of reasons, tried and imprisoned or killed. In many cases, efforts are made to export the ruling ideology to other countries and the ultimate goal is world domination, whether or not this is admitted. In this ambition, no dictator ever fully succeeded, but huge empires were built as starting points for ruling the world.

The following discussion is restricted to the two totalitarian regimes to which Hungary had been exposed from after the First World War until about 1990. The first, often referred to as the Horthy regime, actually went through three phases. At the beginning, during the years 1920–1921, it was a rule of terrorists not fully under control, where anti-Semitism run high, together with violently nationalistic sentiments against the dictates of the Trianon peace treaty. In the second phase, things quieted down and law and order were largely restored. The country was ruled with the help of a two-chamber parliament which even included active opposition parties. Yet, at election time, the outcome was never in doubt. The third phase, after 1939, was marked by increasing Nazi influence and culminated in the German occupation of the country in 1944, and the Arrowcross terror later that year. It seems that, except possibly for the first phase, Horthy was never a true dictator—he was simply not cut out for the role; authoritarian powers were exercised by the governments of the day, some of them extremely right-wing. Yet, it was Horthy's task to select the prime ministers; thus, indirectly, he was responsible for the policies of the successive governments. He appointed such Nazi sympathizers as Imrédy and Bárdossy, the latter leading Hungary into the war, with disastrous end results.

The second totalitarian regime to which Hungary was exposed in the given period was the Communist dictatorship, taking over in 1948. This was a true dictatorship, it was ideology driven and the Russian masters of the regime were obsessed with extending the empire as far as possible. My story and my family's story while we lived under these regimes are given in some detail in the two main parts of this book. Below, a cursory comparison is attempted of the two autocratic regimes, based on our own experience.

All totalitarian regimes regard their citizens in terms of friends and enemies. These groups are defined by the dictators and the ideologies they follow. Dictatorships vastly differ in the treatment of their internal enemies and those whom they consider loyal followers. In Germany, the Nazis regarded all minorities inferior, and treated many in a hostile way. In Hungary, during the middle phase of the Horthy regime, Jews, Communists, freethinkers, and other subversive elements were on the enemy list, and their persecution became much worse, including the obsessive drive to eliminate all Jews, during the German occupation and Arrowcross times. During the socialist regime, enemies included the ex-capitalists (even if they had only two or three employees), rich people in general, ex-Nazis, and those who could not be trusted and were, therefore, considered subversive elements. Our family was definitely in the camp of enemies during the Horthy and Nazi times, and was part of the "acceptable" group for the socialists (although, at the time, I was not always so sure of this). Intellectuals were sometimes respected and at other times regarded with suspicion (see below).

* * *

In the main parts of this book, one can find two words which appear again and again to describe our mental state when times got really bad: *fear* and *stress*. These feelings are, of course, normal parts of everyday life under any circumstances; what was extraordinary was the degree of pressure that caused inordinate amounts of fear and stress, well beyond the levels people can routinely tolerate without suffering damage. Also, one can observe that the Nazis and later the Communist Party had different ways of imposing these dreadful conditions.

During the German and Arrowcross periods, Nazi policies were accepted by a surprising number of Hungarians, perhaps the majority. For these people, living under the Nazis was not particularly stressful. At the same time, for us, the persecuted minority, the death threat was very real—no secret was made of it. Even without being deported or enlisted in a forced labor unit (except for a short period), I came close to being killed a number of times. Hundreds of thousands were actually killed. During the German occupation, in 1944–1945, we lived under constant fear for our lives and the lives of people dear to us—one of the greatest emotional stresses a person can be exposed to.

In contrast, during the socialist years there was, in general, no threat to the life of ordinary people. Once again, the enemies of the regime, the "ex-capitalists," "ex-Nazis," and other "suspicious elements," were harassed in many ways, including having been reduced to filling only inferior jobs, and many of them being deported in 1951. Others were sent to concentration camps, such as the infamous one at Recsk. But, to my knowledge, even this was not an extermination camp (although life was made so miserable there that many, no doubt, wished to die rather than continue to put up with the camp).

Not that the Communist Party shied away from torture and murder[14]. But, in Hungary, common people like us were seldom on the receiving end, and the Party's murderous rages were usually directed against individuals much higher situated on the party or state hierarchy than were we. On the other hand, the entire population was exposed to enormous mental and emotional stresses, particularly during the years before Stalin's death. We had to decide, based on insufficient and distorted information, who were the good guys and, more importantly, who were the bad ones. There was, of course, no such moral dilemma during the Nazi rule. But under the Communists, everybody was suspect, creating an intolerable and, at times, unbearable atmosphere. We were encouraged to inform on friends and parents, all in the name of helping the Party to build a "better world" for future generations. The awful suggestion was to denounce your parents in order to have happy grandchildren.

The rule of the Communist Party was built on fears and stresses, *deliberately* imposed on the population at levels far beyond the normal. Stalin and his representatives in other countries knew very well that maintaining constant fear and high levels of stress was an effective device to keep people in line. An infamous example for such a manipulation was, years later, the momentous Cultural Revolution in China, introduced by Mao Tse-Tung in 1966. While there may have been other reasons, this appeared to be chiefly a response to the notion that the system had become too comfortable, and the people too lax.

---

14 I should make it clear that I am not attempting to provide here a general comparison of the Nazi and the Communist regimes. This would require a far more detailed study. My remarks are more personal: I am comparing the effects these regimes actually had on me and the people around me. It so happened that in Hungary we were exposed to the full horror of the Nazi occupation with deadly consequences for the Jews. For several reasons, the worst of what the Communists were capable of doing did not hit us. To learn more about the latter, one would have to study the history of the Soviet Union in the 1930s.

He ruthlessly uprooted a large part of the population and thereby restored the desired level of fear and stress. One purpose of the Rajk trial was to unbalance even the top party officials.

But stress levels can be too high, even for the purposes of an unyielding dictatorship. Human beings are, in some respects, similar to machines or structures: people, too, can function acceptably only if the stresses to which they are exposed are at tolerable levels. Should the limit of what could be considered tolerable be exceeded for extended periods, most humans would become erratic, and many would break down completely—just like machines would do. Individual tolerance limits are different, and some people may have very high limits; these are the heroes storied in history books, but most ordinary people are not heroes.

To sum up, during the socialist period in Hungary the enemies of the regime did not get the brutal (often bloody) treatment the Nazis routinely administered to their enemies. This was Hitler's obsession, and the mass murders continued well into the period when every resource would have been needed to prop up the war effort. In contrast, there was no mass murder in Hungary during the Socialist period. The enemies were harassed, deported to the countryside, or sent to labor camps but usually not killed. On the other hand, even people who were not considered enemies (a class not much bothered by the Nazis) were regularly stressed emotionally, often beyond their limits. Some of these years, particularly before Stalin's death, were dark for everyone.

A characteristic trait common to both regimes was that they profoundly distrusted intellectuals, people who might solidly support the party line one day and question some of the dogmas the next. Hitler's propaganda chief, Goebbels, declared that he was ready to shoot them, and Stalin made a practice of it. The favorites of both parties had been the conformists, the true followers, who were not capable, or willing, to question the official line. Intellectuals, from St. Paul to Marx, have been indispensable at the stage when new movements were developing their ideologies but, as soon as such a movement came into power, the intellectuals of the day were regularly declared heretics and cheerfully burnt at the stake. Equating nonconformist attitude with subversion has been a widespread practice and not necessarily restricted to dictatorships.

In Hungary, the regimes under discussion treated the intellectuals differently. During the middle period of the Horthy era, the treatment was surprisingly liberal, except for those who were considered subversive, such as the Communists, many of whom were imprisoned. Others lost their jobs and could not find employment. During the ten months of German occupation and Arrowcross terror, there was no identifiable policy regarding intellectuals except for those who were Jewish—they were to be erased from this earth for other reasons: for belonging to an inferior race. During the Communist era, ambitious and enthusiastic intellectuals often made themselves suspicious and regularly got into trouble. Lying low appeared to be the safest policy.

As it was, we lived mostly under dark clouds during both the Nazi and Socialist eras, and at certain times, it was much worse than that. This did not mean that, when the tension was low for a while, there were no relaxed moments or even carefree days. It would have been impossible to go through months or years of tension without periods of at least partial relaxation. However, the nearly unrestricted life and the resulting exuberance, so familiar to young people in the West, were not part of our experience. Only after moving to Canada, and after two or three years of adjustment, did we start to appreciate the difference.

What Could Have Been Done?

This question, whether it would have been possible to resist the Nazis' ruthless roundup and mass murder of Jews, has been briefly touched upon in Part One, and a somewhat broader investigation of the topic is offered below. Imre Kertész in his novel *Fatelessness* (which won him the 2002 Nobel Prize in literature) complained that many who had been victimized in 1944 later recalled the events in the "then came" manner: "Then came the German occupation ... Then came the yellow star ... Then came the designated houses ... Then came the Arrowcross ... Then came the ghetto." Events just seemed to happen to these people, one after the other. And how did they react? Did they just submit to the indignities like sheep? While, sadly, the answer is close to "yes," it triggers other, more difficult questions, such as "What should people have done?" "What could people have done?"

Some of our friends correctly anticipated what was coming and left the country in 1938 when an opportunity arose to obtain Australian visas. For a variety of reasons my family, and most people I knew, didn't do that. The result was that, in 1944, hundreds of thousands of Hungarian Jews were killed. Once the opportunity in 1938 was passed up, very little could have been done to save the Hungarian Jews in 1944.

In his book, *Maskerado* (Cannongate Books, Edinburgh, 2000) Tivadar Soros (father of financier George Soros) describes how he managed to save his family and give help to many others during the German occupation and the Arrowcross times. His philosophy was that since the Jews could not fight Hitler's fury, they must hide from it. So he provided members of his family with false papers and arranged for hiding places where each could stay in comparative safety. However, not every Jewish family included a Tivadar Soros. The necessary ingredients for success were a calm and quick mind not given to despair or panic, connections for obtaining information and also for making the required arrangements, leadership qualities, courage, and money. While Mr. Soros was such a person, people possessing these attributes were rare indeed. And, as Soros was the first to admit, lots of luck was needed, too.

Ironically, Soros would have been much less likely to succeed had a leader like him existed in every Jewish family. It would have been impossible for the entire Jewish community to disappear into hiding without arousing the Nazis' attention and violent response. They would have proceeded to sniff out the Jews in their hiding places and killed those they could find on the spot. So, in a way, Soros's success was based on the fact that the majority of families did *not* have such a leader. Some may feel that there is a moral flaw here, while others would suggest to consider the alternative before making judgment. In the latter light, Mr. Soros was quite right in suggesting that all families in a position to make the necessary arrangements should disappear into hiding. These families would still have accounted for only a small proportion of the Jewish community.

In general, the morality of a proposed solution where a part of the community is favored but not the rest depends on the foreseeable fate of the rest. If, as a consequence, the rest is likely to endure extra suffering the solution appears surely immoral. If the rest would not likely be affected by a favor extended to a group, the solution should not be regarded unethical.[15] It is very difficult to make prior estimates of these

---

15 These principles can be taken to the extreme. In his famous book, *Lashik Roitschwanz* (1928), Ilya Ehrenburg describes an incident when the leader of a Jewish community becomes so cozy with God that he dares to ask for reducing the human suffering of his community. But, as he looks down, he sees that after

chances, and I would hesitate to blame Andrew Elek's grandfather for his policies regarding the Budapest Jews (see Part One). And I doubt that by spreading the word about Auschwitz, at great peril to himself and the messengers, he could have saved many Jews in the provinces.

This is the scenario widely known and most often debated: the Jewish Council knew about Auschwitz but withheld this information so as to prevent foreseeable and unforeseeable evil consequences. Another version of what happened is described by Sir Martin Gilbert, a noted authority on the holocaust. According to this, Eichmann offered the Jewish Council the choice of saving all Hungarian Jews for 10,000 trucks and given amounts of commodities; otherwise, he was quite prepared to kill them. A delegate was dispatched to Istanbul to start negotiations with the Allies. Eichmann assured the Council that during the talks deportations would proceed but only to a "holding camp" where the inmates would be treated humanely. On signing the agreement, those in the camp would be transferred to a neutral country. However, this was part of a large-scale deception: in fact, the Jews were immediately delivered to Auschwitz where over 400,000 of them were killed. Eichmann was a master manipulator. The news reached the Allies and several neutral countries, causing such an international outcry[16] that Horthy felt compelled to halt the deportation of the remaining Budapest Jews, about 120,000 in total. This scenario does not put any blame on members of the Council; it regards them all as victims of Eichmann's deceptive promises.

* * *

---

a long fast his people are becoming weak and one, an old man, is near dying. He interrupts his bargaining with God and returns to the earth to end the fast and save the old man. He refuses to offer the life of even a single person in order to make the life of everyone else better.

16 President Roosevelt in an extremely strongly worded ultimatum declared that "Hungary's fate will not be like any other civilized nation['s] ... unless the deportations are stopped." (Hannah Arendt, *Eichmann in Jerusalem*, Penguin Books, 1977, p. 201).

Saving the entire community was not something Eichmann could have been expected to do - his mandate was to exterminate all Jews in Europe. Over the times, many people believed that organized resistance by members of a large community could be the only effective approach for the purpose. In practice, however, this solution did not have a good record of success; for example, in one of the best-known efforts, the Jews in Warsaw tried it, and failed. Individual family decisions were often successful in saving the family, but had all families acted at the same time, in a random fashion or in an organized way (a near-impossible scenario), this would have likely led to a major catastrophe.

Instead, I am inclined to agree with Prof. István Deák, known expert of central and eastern European history and politics, who suggested that: "… only one institution could have prevented the Hungarian Holocaust, and that is the Hungarian state …" (letter of 2010-02-28). During the German occupation of Hungary, such a state intervention did indeed happen, but only once, when Admiral Horthy prevented the deportation of the Budapest Jews (described in Part 1). This was the more remarkable because, to my knowledge, among the Nazi-occupied countries Hungary was perhaps the only one with an independent army, under the Regent's command, which could successfully stand up to the Germans and force them to change their plans.

One can only speculate how history would have evolved if, in 1941, Horthy had shown the same determination, and would have chosen someone less devoted to Nazi policies than László Bárdossy, as the prime minister to succeed Count Teleki. With more firmness and involvement,[17] Horthy could have possibly prevented, or at least significantly delayed the country's entrance into the war. In doing so, he could have saved a large number of soldiers of the soon to be defeated

---

17 Horthy's own, somewhat self-serving but fascinating account of how Hungary entered the war is contained in Chapter 17 of his memoirs (Admiral N. Horthy, *Memoirs,* Hutchinson, London, 1957. A new edition, annotated by Horthy's daughter-in-law, whose views were far to the left from those by the Regent, appeared in 2000).

2nd army on the Russian front, and also many Jews in the auxiliary units accompanying the army.

The additional number of years for which Hungary could have stayed neutral is difficult to guess; it is safe to assume that the latest when Germany would have occupied the country would have been around the same time when they actually did it, in March 1944. The number of Jews in the provinces deported and mass murdered, actions which started soon after the occupation, could have been at least significantly reduced by Horthy taking a very firm stand against it. However, the enthusiastic collaboration with the Germans of the new Sztójay government, and of all at lower levels who participated in the local organization of the deportations with great zeal, made it sure that they were carried out smoothly and efficiently, allowing Horthy to assume a passive attitude for a while. Only months later did international protests (see footnote 16, p. 129) convince him to stand up for the Budapest Jews.

In the German-controlled areas, there were only a handful of successful efforts to save Jewish lives on a large scale. Perhaps the best-known was the organized action in Denmark to save all the Jews by smuggling them to neutral Sweden. But allegedly the state's hand was in it, and the occupying Germans seemed to look the other way; for once preferring economic cooperation to the eradication of Jews.[18]

Another incident was the delivery of about 1700 Hungarian Jews by train to Switzerland, as a result of somewhat shady negotiations

---

18 In two other countries, Bulgaria and Italy, there were no widespread anti-Semitic sentiments and these governments could resist much of the time the German pressure to round up and deport the Jews.

The Bulgarian story is of particular interest. When, after repeated German demands, the final ultimatum was issued in March 1943 to collect and deport the Jews to Nazi camps, the Bulgarian parliament voted against it, and on the selected day the King rode out to the streets in full regalia, adding to his rows of decorations a new one, the yellow star of David. Also, the Bishop Metropolitan Kiril of Plovdiv is said to have selected a suitable spot along the rail line where the train carrying the Jews would proceed and stood across the tracks, forcing the train to stop. The deportations didn't occur that day, or on any other day later.

between the German authorities and a courageous lawyer and Zionist leader, Rezső Kasztner. There were bribes involved, bluffing was going on by both sides, the transfers were far from smooth, but the action was finally successful.[19] Yet this affected only a small group, a far cry from the entire community.

Significant actions were also carried out by groups of young Zionists. They concentrated not so much on confronting the Germans, but on saving lives. These activities included equipping Jews with false papers and smuggling such Jewish groups to safer countries such as Romania from where many could continue to Palestine. They were also busy with making arrangements for safe camps for children. These activities have been described in several papers, such as the one in the footnote[20], including further references.

Until the onset of the Arrowcross regime and terror in October 1944, very little organized effort was evident to protect the remaining Jews in Budapest. From August, the Swedish and Swiss Embassies started issuing letters of protection to individuals; these documents were much sought after because it was believed that owners of such letters would be exempt should a new wave of deportations occur. Once the Arrowcross took over, the Swedish and Swiss activities became highly significant, joined by similar steps taken by the Vatican, Spain and Portugal. Protective passes were distributed by the thousands, originals joined by many forged

---

19 A detailed description of the incident is given in the book *Kasztner's Train,* by Anna Porter (Douglas & McIntyre, 2007). The fateful events during the spring and summer of 1944 have been discussed in a large number of documents; such as in a long essay by the foremost expert of the era, Randolph L. Braham, titled *Rescue Operations in Hungary: Myths and Realities* (East European Quarterly, Summer 2004, p. 173.)

20 David Gur: *Resistance and Rescue Operations by the Hungarian Zionist Youth Movement in 1944.* Published by the Society for the Research of the History of the Zionist Youth Movement in Hungary, Ramat Gan, Israel, June 2009.

I am indebted to Mr Ronny Lustig for making this and other references available to me. Mr Lustig is a director of the Memorial Museum of Hungarian Speaking Jewry (founded by his parents) in Safed, Israel.

ones. Protected houses were established for those with protective passes. Heroes emerged, like the legendary Swedish diplomat Raoul Wallenberg who at great risk to his own life personally appeared in camps from where it was planned to march the captives, mostly women and old people, to the Austrian border, often on foot. By handing out passes and arguing his case with the armed thugs, he regularly managed to free many victims and escorted them back to the city.

The Swiss Consulate dealing with emigration, a department of the Embassy, was led by Consul Carl Lutz and headquartered in a former glass panel dealership on Vadász Street, popularly called the glass house. Their actions were less spectacular but equally effective. The glass house sheltered nearly two thousand Jews, including many Zionists, and also other refugees; attacks on protected houses by Nazi thugs were often successfully neutralized by people from the Consulate promptly appearing on the scene. They saved my life twice.

At the beginning, my family's attitude and that of many of our friends, was completely passive. By appearing invisible, we hoped to survive. Both in 1944 and 1956, the necessity for active self-protection occurred to us only late, in the cathartic, lawless end periods. The tentative steps we took in 1944 are recounted in Part One of this book. Most of these, however, were improvised, ad-hoc actions, not parts of thought-through plans, such as arranging for hiding places for all in the family; we just did not comprehend the nature of the danger. It was mostly sheer luck that saved us. In 1956, our successful escape to Austria was, in contrast, based on much community information.

There is no doubt that preparing and being ready to follow emergency plans is preferable for a family to an attitude of meek submission to hostile powers. Actions based on such plans can save many lives. Plans for entire communities appear still risky.

What Did Actually Happen?

While we may have thought we knew, we didn't know and couldn't even guess what was in fact happening. We moved into a Swiss-protected house in mid-November and were surprised to see that during frequent raids the Arowcross thugs removed all those who didn't have a letter of protection issued by the Swiss Consulate. We figured it was the job of the protectors to make sure that all living in a "protected" building should have a valid pass. But we didn't know why the real events occurred.

The fact was that our building was part of a ghetto situated on the Pest-side of the Danube, across the Margit Island. Because most houses were protected by foreign Embassies, this ghetto became known as the "international" ghetto. Since it was small (just a few blocks, perhaps 30), it was limited in the number of Jews it could accommodate, and according to the original "vision" of the Arrowcross a much bigger ghetto was needed. The walls of this, made of wooden planks, were built in November; and early in December its four gates were closed, and the ghetto was ready for operation. It extended from the Central Synagogue in the South to almost the Large Ring Boulevard in the North, and from Király Street to Dohány Street in the West-Easterly Direction. It was estimated that the two ghettos together could hold about 100 000 Jews. Since the goal was to have all Jews in the city stay in the ghettos, the above arrangement seemed to have served the purpose: it helped to make the remainder of the city *"judenfrei"* – free of

Jews. Why was this so important we didn't understand – but we didn't concentrate on such questions, our minds were full of daily problems, and our hopes were that the Soviet Army would soon occupy both ghettos, ending our misery (see Part 1).

Only years later could we read about the full story[21], and it was not a cheerful reading. It was Hitler's old obsession that the Jewish Question (JQ), the intolerable presence of Jews in Europe, need to be solved in one way or another. His original idea was, in the 1920's, to transport all the Jews to some remote island (if I correctly recall, Madagascar was often mentioned, where, he thought, there was enough space for the purpose). When this didn't turn out to be a practical possibility for the Final Solution (FS) of the JQ, he simply conceived the idea of "erasing" all Jews in Europe (*ausradieren,* one of Hitler's favorite expressions in his speeches). The details of the program were established during the infamous conference in January 1942 at the Wannsee Villa in Berlin. Participants at the conference represented the German Government, the Nazi Party, the army, ministries and other relevant agencies. The construction of the Budapest ghettos in 1944 became apparently part of the FS.

Details of the FS were closely-guarded secrets, and very few knew anything about them, the Jews in the last place. The undermining of the bridges across the Danube and of the ghettos (if the latter was ever fully done) was not known in advance, and never discussed. Yet, the situation was becoming increasingly grim. About the FS regarding the Jews, details did leak out to a few people, including an Arrowcross/police liaison officer, Pál Szalai, who felt less than happy with the proposed plan for the extermination of all Jews in town. So, he devised his own agenda to try to stop the massacre, and showed it to Wallenberg, who fully agreed. The next day or so, Szalai visited the person who would be responsible for giving the signal to blow up the ghettos, the German

---

21 Most of the following information is based on the excellent book by Krisztián Ungváry, *The Siege of Budapest – 100 Days in World War II* (English edition: Yale University Press, 2005).

General Gerhard Schmidhuber who commanded a German panzer division on the Pest side. Szalai quietly explained it to him that, after the war, as a commander he would be held responsible for all actions of his subordinates.

The General took this warning extremely seriously. He invited to a meeting his leading officers, a few Arrowcross ministers, and others whose presence he considered necessary, and announced that he was forbidding the massacre. Also, he was sending out a few SS units to make sure that his orders were properly carried out.

The ghettos were not blown up. The lives of more than 90 000 Jews were saved; fewer than the 100 000 mentioned before, mainly because of the activities of Arrowcross thugs who in December and early in January nightly descended on one or two of the protected houses in the "international" district and killed all inhabitants by machine-gunning them into the nearby Danube which already started to freeze up (see Part 1). Also in the same period, a large number of Jews were murdered at random in the ghettos and elsewhere in the city.

* * *

Again, it was a miracle! It was the greatest of all miracles I had experienced during my odyssey through that incredible era in the years 1944 – 1945. Every time I talk about this miracle, write about it, or only think about it, my eyes get filled with tears. After all, it was the moment that gave tens of thousands, including me, a chance for a new life – based on a split second's decision!

Printed in the United States
By Bookmasters